Light on Enlightenment

Light on Enlightenment

Revolutionary Teachings on the Inner Life

Christopher Titmuss

SHAMBHALA
Boston
1999

SHAMBHALA PUBLICATIONS, INC.
Horticultural Hall
300 Massachusetts Avenue
Boston, Massachusetts 02115
www.shambhala.com

©1998 by Christopher Titmuss
Published by arrangement with Rider, an imprint of
Ebury Press, Random House, London.

9 8 7 6 5 4 3 2 1
FIRST SHAMBHALA EDITION

Printed in the United States of America

⊗ This edition is printed on acid-free paper that meets the
American National Standards Institute Z39.48 Standard.

Distributed in the United States by Random House, Inc.,
and in Canada by Random House of Canada Ltd

Library of Congress Cataloging-in-Publication Data

Titmuss, Christopher.
    Light on enlightenment: revolutionary teachings of
the inner life/by Christopher Titmuss.—1st ed.
        p. cm.
    Originally published: London: Rider, 1998.
    ISBN 1-57062-514-X (pbk.: alk. paper)
    1. Buddhism—Doctrines—Introductions. I. Title.
BQ4132.T58   1999
294.3'4—dc21   99-34790
                                                      CIP

CONTENTS

FIVE PRECEPTS

FOUR DIVINE ABIDINGS

FOUR ABSORPTIONS

FOUR FORMLESS REALMS

FOUR NOBLE ONES

ACKNOWLEDGEMENTS

I wish to express my deepest appreciation to the Buddha, the Dharma and the Sangha. The influence of the Buddha runs throughout the pages of this book. I believe that what is stated in this book keeps entirely faithful with the core message of the Buddha – that enlightenment is accessible here and now to men and women who aspire to such a noble realisation. I have experienced a daily connection with the Dharma since 1967.

I wish to express gratitude to Venerable Ajahn Dhammadharo (b.1914), Abbot of Wat Sai Ngam (Monastery of Beautiful Banyan Trees), Supanburi, Thailand. I spent more than half of my six years as a Buddhist monk under his guidance in Insight (Vipassana) Meditation.

I wish to express gratitude to Venerable Ajahn Buddhadasa (1907–1993) of Wat Suanmoke (Monastery of the Garden of Liberation), Chai Ya, Surat Thani, Thailand. He made clear the importance of full liberation through utter non-attachment.

Sharda Rogell edited *Light on Enlightenment*. No one was better qualified. We have been teaching the Dharma together world-wide since the mid-1980s. She is thoroughly familiar with my teaching and ways of working with people. Her encouragement, advice and suggestions have been invaluable in the writing of this book. Special thanks, too, to Gill Farrer-Halls for reading the typescript through.

I would like to thank Judith Kendra of Rider Books for encouraging me to submit a Dharma book and for her support throughout the project, and also Julia Macrae and Jane Birdsell for working on the text for the publishers. I would also like to thank various friends who have come to my home regularly to help with office and household tasks while I wrote the book. They include Janey Francis, Jacquie Kilty, Peter McGahon, Sue Milner, Lorraine Wood and Liah Woodward. They continue to be a great support.

I wish to thank Nshorna, my daughter, for her wonderful presence; also Gwanwyn Williams, my mother, and my late father for their kindness. Also thanks to all those who support Gaia House, our retreat centre in south Devon, England.

Since the mid-1970s, I have been teaching annual retreats in Bodh Gaya, India, where the Buddha was enlightened. I wish to express a special thank-you to the Lord Abbot of the Thai Monastery, Bodh Gaya, for making his monastery available for the retreats. *The Middle Length Discourses of the Buddha*, beautifully translated by Bhikkhu Nanamoli and Bhikkhu Bodhi and published by Wisdom Books, Boston, USA, has been an invaluable resource in the writing of this book.

In the book there are a number of stories of people's experiences. I have changed the names of all those concerned, and occasionally one or two details, out of respect for their circumstances. I refer to some themes, such as awareness, dependent arising of conditions, *I* and *my*, meditation, liberation and enlightenment, regularly throughout the book. The Buddhist tradition has used repetition in texts to remind readers of the essential teachings. Some of the themes in this book have been expanded upon in two of my previous books, *The Profound and the Profane* and *The Green Buddha*.

Finally, thank you to countless people around the world who enable me to serve the Dharma. There is no greater privilege.

May all beings live in peace.
May all beings live in harmony.
May all beings be fully enlightened.

The Buddha's Charter for Inquiry

THE KALAMA PEOPLE: 'How are we to know which person who addresses us is telling the truth?'

THE BUDDHA: 'Do not accept anything because

1. Of repeated oral transmission.
2. Of lineage or tradition.
3. It has been widely stated.
4. It has been written in books, such as scriptures.
5. It is logical and reasonable.
6. Of inferring and drawing conclusions.
7. It has been thought out.
8. Of acceptance and conviction through a theory.
9. The speaker appears competent.
10. Of respect for the teacher.

Know what things would be censured by the wise and which, if pursued, would lead to harm and suffering.'

INTRODUCTION

What The School Taught
What The Enlightened One Taught

I was lucky enough to leave school at the age of fifteen years and eight months, never to go back. In the last year of attending the John Fisher Roman Catholic Boys' School , Purley, England, I took very little interest in my studies or exams and finished near the bottom of the class. I left school without a single educational qualification. It seemed to me then that school endeavoured to minimise one's enjoyment of life, of fun and play. It wasn't worth the sacrifice.

Years later in a remote Buddhist monastery in Southeast Asia, I recalled one event at school. It was the daily ritual of caning. The works of the Buddha came to mind when he said, 'I declare there is suffering and there is the resolution of suffering.' His words brought tears to my eyes when I reflected on the needless suffering that boys in the school went through.

I remembered that upon leaving school I held the school record for the number of canings, a total of one hundred and eight strokes in less than four years. I don't recall committing any major offences. Apart from failing to do wretched homework, I specialised in pranks. Unscrewing the master's desk so that it collapsed when he leaned on it. Leaving old smoked haddock under the floorboards so the classroom stank. Writing graffiti and sending paper darts flying through the air as the teacher wrote on the blackboard.

The school provided a small room for a humourless teacher, a certain Mr Fleming, who handed out the caning daily, either at noon or 3.30 p.m. The cane was in fact a whale-bone covered in leather. Punishment consisted of two strokes, four strokes, six strokes or eight strokes. Or double eight. But nobody ever got double eight, not even me.

1

I can recall the fear and terror that we boys experienced as we queued outside the room for our respective punishments. Some whimpered as they heard the *whoosh* of the whalebone strike across the palm of the hand of the boy in the room. Occasionally, we would hear Mr Fleming yelling at a boy to keep still if that boy, stricken with fear, pulled his hand back or suddenly lowered it when the cane came down. Clearly, the values of the Middle Ages still held sway then in many English schools.

I far preferred to be caned than to have the monotony of writing out hundreds of times. 'I shall not make a nuisance of myself in the classroom.' After the strokes, I simply blew warm breath on the palms of my hands for several minutes until the painful sensations faded away. Then it was over. One could see that for other boys the terror and humiliation hurt more than the strokes on the hand.

I still have sympathy for that expression of extreme thought which says we only stop learning when we go to school. I greatly appreciate the immense significance of education – to learn to read, write, add and subtract is to gain some of the most powerful tools available to a human being. Education is a marvellous and indispensable tool for inner development but I believe it still remains often out of touch with the depths of inner experience and the wisdom of the heart. The Latin word *educat* means 'to lead out', 'to bring out'. Whether schools truly fulfill that mission is questionable.

It was rather ironic that thirty years after leaving school, I was invited to speak at a conference on the *Philosophy of the Future of Humanity* at Cambridge University. There I expressed the view that education easily abuses the mind through imposing on it too many demands to absorb knowledge, to be clever, to be ruthlessly self-interested. The desire to add letters before and after one's name seems to imply that students are not satisfied with the number of letters in their name! To live wisely and intelligently requires a deep, meditative re-examination of priorities. Without this inquiry, we will go on demanding more and more from the minds of the young to force them to fit into the objectives of the private and public sector.

After I left school I got a job as an office boy for a weekly paper called *The Universe*. It sounds very cosmic but in fact it was a popular newspaper for the country's Roman Catholics. The newspaper didn't move away from the traditional teachings of the Church. But when Pope John XX111 became Pope in 1958 he opened up the doors of the Church to re-examine its place in the contemporary world. He was a breath of fresh air.

As an eighteen-year-old I could not appreciate fully the changes to the Church since I preferred my BSA Super Road Rocket 650cc motorbike with its lowered handlebars, rear-set footrests, and sponge fixed to the top of the tank for my chin to rest on to maximise speed. It is an uncanny matter of existence that our love of freedom does not necessarily fit comfortably with our institutions. There seemed to be a greater freedom on the motorbike than in the salvation that the Church offered.

At the age of twenty-two, I quit my second job as a London journalist with the *Irish Independent* newspaper, crossed the Channel, and headed east with the princely sum of £50 in my pocket. My parents thought I was foolish to throw away a promising career to go hitch-hiking around the world. I loved them so I said I would not be away from home for long. In fact, it was ten years and ten days before I returned to England, having kept travelling east until I got back home without turning around.

After three years of living out of a backpack, I abandoned it in Thailand for six years of the begging bowl, brown robes, shaved head and bare feet of a Buddhist monk. I soon realised that the outer journeys of life are small change compared to the challenge of the inner journey and what that demands from us. Very occasionally Western missionaries would come to our monastery from outlying villages where they attempted to convert the local Buddhists and Muslims. Mercifully, not with much success!

The missionaries demanded to know why I had become a Buddhist and abandoned my Christian faith. I told them Jesus sent me. They were not amused. And I was not trying to be funny. I regarded Jesus as an inspirational, free and enlightened person, a Jewish rabbi whose passion for life couldn't be quenched. I believed he would have applauded my commitment to shake off the yoke of the past, of the unhealthy aspects of Western conditioning, and explore the down-to-earth teachings of the Buddha.

I still believe the Buddha's teachings rank as the most comprehensive message of the awakening available to humanity. I should add here that I am not a Buddhist. I have no appetite for labels.

Neither am I concerned with the promotion of the religion. That's not my cup of tea. Yet I believe the Buddhist tradition offers a genuine education about life.

In the early 1980s in Devon, England, I became the co-founder of Gaia House, an international retreat centre offering teachings and practices dedicated to liberation, inquiry and insight meditation. There is a hunger in society for teachings and practices that apply directly to the realities of daily life. I believe that this book addresses those realities in a clear and straightforward manner, and I hope it will be used as a resource for clarity, inquiry, and for discovering an enlightened life. The issues I have addressed apply as long as men and women walk on this earth, and the book can be read and re-read by the individual and in group discussions to explore the truths of daily existence.

I am asked with alarming regularity why I eventually disrobed. Was I disillusioned? The thought arose at that time, 'When the fruit is ripe it has to leave the tree.' That's not intended to be a conceited statement. It was time to change. Sometimes our freedom expresses the ending of one form of relationship and the start or return to another. That does not mean to say that we believe we are moving to something better and getting rid of something bad.

This book reminds us of deep truths that we may have forgotten or need to attend to. It attempts to communicate in clear and practical terms the message of enlightenment. The Buddha had one clear intention throughout his forty-five years of teaching: he sought to enlighten human experience and end, once and for all, the daily problems common to humanity.

The Buddha gave bold, uncompromising teachings which he referred to as the *Dharma*, an ancient Sanskrit word that also means 'duty'. He frequently made it plain that our primary duty expresses the determination to discover insights into life, to penetrate into the notion of self-existence and realise the joy of freedom.

For a hundred generations, that is around 2,500 years, the teachings of the Buddha stayed in the East. Then the teachings began taking firm root in the West. Some of the responsibility for that belongs to Westerners who journeyed to the East to listen, practise and realise the teachings of the Buddha, and some of the responsibility belongs to Asian teachers travelling to the West. Some Westerners returned to the West to teach the Dharma.

The teachings examined in this book address every feature of our lives. They are profound teachings intended for thoughtful men and women wishing to uncover the veils of existence. They are for people who sense that life is neither blindly mechanistic, nor inherently benign, neither destructive nor in the hands of a Supreme Figure. The Buddha taught the Middle Way which points to the ground between self-hate and self-infatuation, between notions of free choice and inner latent forces. The question of who we are and what we are is one of his many concerns.

The Buddha's teachings never fall comfortably into a single convenient category, nor did he intend them to. One can hardly call the Dharma a religion when the Buddha took no interest in temples, religious worship, belief in God or soul. There is a relationship between Buddhism and the Dharma which has been insightful – and sectarian through clinging to views. The Theravada and Mahayana Buddhist traditions originally consisted of commentaries on the same early texts of the Buddha's teachings that I am using. Some Buddhist schools have replaced devotion to God with guru devotion, hymns with chanting, and liberation with fretting about rebirth.

Neither can one place Buddhist teachings into philosophy. The Buddha questioned again and again views, opinions, intellectual cleverness and infatuation with ideas. Western academics and students show an increasing degree of interest in the Dharma but mostly from a cerebral standpoint rather than from their day-to-day experience and practice.

Nor can the teachings fit into the field of psychotherapy, which relies mostly on the exchange of language between therapist and client to understand *certain* features of the make-up of the personality. Generally speaking, psychotherapy examines issues of self involved in relationship to matters past, present or future. Psychotherapy explores our attitudes, certain states of mind and the impact of others upon our lives. A tradition that is barely a century old cannot expect to have the same depth of experience and realisation as a tradition 2,500 years old triggered by a profound and unstoppable awakening.

I believe neither religion, study nor therapy goes far enough, nor deep enough, into the nature of existence. Many in those respected fields would also agree.

Yet devotion, analysis and personal issues do deserve care and attention. At times, these approaches offer support for living reasonably well-adjusted lives. They can provide an invaluable resource for inner well-being and, for some, point to something deep and profound. If we are willing to take risks for change we might gain wonderful and illuminating insights into this infinitely varied field of existence.

In that respect the Dharma is a beautiful teaching embracing far-reaching ethical values, significant depths of meditation, healing of the heart, and profound wisdom while also pointing directly to an enlightened life. The Buddha himself said that only those who see the Dharma see the Buddha. To be enlightened is to see the Buddha. There is no fading away of an authentically enlightened life since it sets the vision and direction of our own lives.

I have attempted to cut through the superficial face of the religion of Buddhism to reveal the indispensable features of the Dharma. Originally – for ten or fifteen generations – the teachings were transmitted orally. Rather skilfully, the Buddha drew together the priorities for enlightenment into small lists, which made them easy to remember and easy to transmit orally. His approached worked. This book consists of a short commentary on each of the primary topics that the Buddha emphasised, beginning with the Four Noble Truths. Commentary on primary texts is a tradition that goes back more than two thousand years. The epigraphs above each chapter are poetic meditations on these topics.

It is my intention that readers have a through and comprehensive picture of what it means to make the journey to enlightenment. Let no one ever deceive you into believing that enlightenment is a quiet, sublime state of mind or a sudden moment that fades into personal history. Enlightenment is one with the truth of things. It never fades. It requires the enlivening of every resource available, inwardly and outwardly.

Enlightened people who have skills in communication only point the way, but human beings must walk the path. To step out in this direction may create ripples, if not waves, not only in our lives but also for others as well. To face our existence, to focus on the Threefold Inner Training of morality, depths of meditation, and wisdom, will challenge the very core of our being. The discipline of the Dharma will have an impact on our views of our values, career and future prospects if these are charged with egotism and self-delusion. The Dharma confronts the supreme value of the West, namely the elevation of the self.

This book serves as a guide away from the world of possessiveness, clinging and egotism to the awakening of the heart and a clear perception of the nature of things. Enlightening our existence puts our brief exposure on this earth into another realm of understanding altogether.

In the Dharma,
Christopher Titmuss
Totnes, Devon,
UK

May all beings live in peace and harmony.
May all beings be liberated.
May all beings be fully enlightened.

THE FOUR
NOBLE TRUTHS

When this force of ego moves upon the present,
I am blinded to the consequences,
To the slavery of its movement,
That takes no account of what abides
In receptivity all around.

Introduction

The Four Noble Truths are:

1. There is suffering.
2. Desire is a cause of suffering.
3. There is liberation from suffering.
4. There is the Path to Liberation.

The Four Noble Truths express the hub of the teachings. All the remaining teachings act like spokes in the Wheel of the Dharma. All subsequent teachings and practices point to one or more of the Four Noble Truths in countless ways. Non religious, non philosophical, the Truths address the core issues of daily existence. They are neither positive nor negative. They reveal the way things are. We have the capacity to change what needs to change and accept what needs accepting. It is an enormous challenge to investigate what living is all about.

The teachings point directly to the transformation of all levels of suffering, depths of insight into our existence, and the joy of liberation. Each one of the Four Noble Truths reminds us directly

8

of what really matters in life.

The conventional mind would say the logical order for the Four Noble Truths ought to be Suffering, Causes, the Path and Liberation instead of Suffering, Causes, Liberation and the Path. The order is the right one. We can realise the cessation of suffering conclusively in a moment. If we do not see the liberating truth clearly, then we develop every factor of the Eightfold Path, dealt with in the next chapter, until we see clearly.

When we see Nirvana, that is the unshakeable joy of freedom, we live the Noble Eightfold Path. Before this realisation we cultivate the Path to Liberation (which is Enlightenment). After realisation, the Path dissolves. The Noble Ones make noble all of the eight links. All the teachings point to full realisation of this noble way of being in this world.

I regard these teachings as revolutionary since they call upon us to look into every single facet of our existence and our impact upon the world. They challenge us to awaken while in the midst of everyday circumstances. Nothing is ignored. We have the potential to enlighten our life without going to a monastery or to meditate in a cave. Instead of submitting to the ups and downs of daily life, we start by bringing our awareness to bear on our inner life. It is the first step towards full enlightenment.

Suffering

Why is there all this emphasis on suffering in Buddhism? Many thoughtful people will look at their own lives and the lives of people close to them and wonder why Buddhists make such a fuss about it.

Of course there is suffering. Unimaginable suffering. We only have to watch the television news to hear horrifying accounts of the kinds of suffering taking place in this world. Happy news items do get broadcast but they are infrequent – a royal wedding, a big lottery winner, a successful manned flight into space.

To dwell on all the suffering and the depths of inhumanity and depravity that people express towards each other seems morbid and depressing. We might rightly conclude that there is enough despair and cynicism in the world already. So what are the Buddhists going on about?

The reference point for Buddhists hangs on a Pali (the language that records the Buddha's teachings) word, *dukkha*. It means *suffering* but also includes the entire range of *unsatisfactory* experiences. These forms of experience can relentlessly haunt our life. Success and failure, hopes and fears, ups and downs, upset the balance of our lives. We would love to be able to resolve this situation but we don't know how.

The Dharma, namely that which sheds light on enlightenment, offers the practical resources possible to resolve the problems of existence. Every one of them. There are plenty of people who live well-adjusted lives. Their emotional life is in good order, they have a good home life, good job and good friends. Ask such people 'How's life?' Their immediate response is, 'Life is good.' So it might be. Yet many people, even with all the success in the world, do not feel satisfied. They have everything – emotional and physical health, financial security – and yet they continue to feel dissatisfied. The fact that others say they would give an arm and a leg to be in their position doesn't stop them from feeling that ultimately nothing is really satisfying. Even though they have nothing to complain about, they know in their heart of hearts they remain unfulfilled. This is *dukkha*. The practice and the teachings aim to resolve this *dukkha* completely. It is no idle claim.

In East and West, too many Buddhists view life as suffering. They take a rather depressed view of existence. Rather than admit that, they'll claim that the Buddha declared, 'Life is suffering.' He didn't. Such a phrase never appears in the volumes of teachings attributed to the Buddha. But that has never stopped certain Buddhists from claiming that he did. He refutes stridently such nihilistic views. It is hardly surprising that Buddhists who cling to these views are attracted to personal extinction which they claim is Nirvana.

The Buddha states that the Second Noble Truth (which is the cause of suffering) arises when the conditions are there for it to arise. Suffering cannot arise when the conditions are not there for its dependent arising. He urges us to give attention to this, to meditate and reflect on it for direct insight into the way things are. His view is neither pessimistic nor optimistic, but realistic. He would consider it crude to proclaim such a grossly generalised statement as 'Life is suffering.'

Any feature of life can become associated with suffering. A royal wedding can become a bitter divorce, a lottery win can become a nightmare for a whole family, a flight into space can become filled with terror or worse. In trying to make sense of this, we can blame God, change, destiny, others or ourselves. But this rarely brings relief.

Birth, ageing, pain and death commonly mean exposure to some degree of suffering and can bring anguish to our loved ones. It seems we often forget that birth invites ageing, pain and death whether we live a day or a hundred years. In some Buddhist countries, people recite, 'Birth, ageing, pain and death' with mantra-like regularity so that they never forget that existence includes all four. Immortality of the body belongs to fanciful thinking. Why must we die? Because we are born. It's that basic. Mercifully it is not the whole truth, as will become apparent.

The worst form of suffering is hell. Famines, wars, forces of destruction, torture chambers, experiments on animals, desecration of nature, reveal hell on earth. We have no need to look any further. Yet hell also resides in the human psyche in its tortured and fragmented state. Hell is the terror of the unknown and the tyranny of the known. For some there is no escape from hell owing to the impersonal forces that sentient creatures endure from within and without.

Hell can be known in this life or in other planes of existence. Hell manifests as a severe mental disorder. It is being trapped in the realm of suffering without knowing a way out. Besieged with torment, the individual knows neither the means nor possibility of escape from their circumstances, inner or outer. There seems to be nobody around who understands, nor who can help, except to offer platitudes and medication. This is hell.

Fortunately, heaven also exists on earth and heaven is discoverable from within. Bliss, joy and sublime happiness reveal heaven. Heaven shows itself in love and intimacy of human contact, in the ecstatic feeling of connection and fulfilment. Heaven shows itself in the wonders of nature, from the vastness of the night sky to the unfolding of a flower on a magical day. Heaven is in the mystical experience and the sense of wonder.

Heaven and hell share common characteristics: they are both subject to arising and passing away. We may feel overwhelming relief when hell ends, and a sense of loss and disappointment when we depart from heaven. There is nothing permanent about these experiences and the self cannot produce them at will. It seems our life can move between heaven and hell and the ordinariness of human activity. Satisfaction and dissatisfaction become associated with the realms of heaven, hell and in-between. Unless we truly understand our relationship to ourselves, others, places and things, and the cycle of events between birth and death, we will define life via pleasure and pain.

Between 1970 and 1976 I was an ordained Buddhist monk in Thailand and India. For the first three years I stayed in one monastery, Wat Chai Na, in Nakornsridhammaraj (Wat Chai Na means Monastery at the End of the Rice Paddy. Nakornsridhammaraj means City of the Kings of Dharma). The monastery was about fifteen hours by train south from Bangkok, in a province with many terrorists. For a long time, I was the only Western monk within three or four hours of the monastery. Being English and somewhat slow to learn a foreign language meant that I spent much of this time in utter silence, living in a hut and meditating under the trees day and night.

During the first year, a kindly Indian monk, Bhikkhu Nagasena translated the evening talks to the monks and nuns of the teacher, Ajahn Dhammadharo, and also my personal meetings with him. After Ven. Nagasena returned to Bangkok, I had to wait for the occasional English-speaking Asian monk or visiting Western monk to come to the monastery, so that I could speak with the teacher.

It was a rather severe, disciplined way of life. The teacher rejected study, books, daily chanting and conversational life. There was a single message. Meditate. Face your existence. Look at your stuff. Awaken your heart. Realise liberation.

By conventional standards, some would call such a way of life hell on earth, or at least purgatory. In the voluntary deprivation of life's comforts, I either had to go deep within myself to touch the mysterious and profound, or call it a day. Throughout the year I engaged in standing meditation every day, under a tree, for three hours from noon to 3 p.m. Along with sitting and walking meditation, the standing meditation became a resource for insights. Some would regard such a daily routine as extreme but I got into the rhythm and flow of using the postures of sitting, walking, standing and reclining. They contributed to a grounding in the depth of the immediacy of things and the seeing into the nature of the here and now.

The Buddha disputes the common view that the pursuit of pleasure makes life worthwhile. Instead, he says the depths of meditation, the joy of awareness, the opening of the heart and enlightening the mind bring fulfilment.

Our practice includes learning to stand steady and clear in the face of change since much suffering arises through:

1. Not getting what we want.

2. Losing what we have.

3. Being separated from what we love.

4. Clinging and attachment to material forms, feelings, perceptions, mental states including thoughts, and consciousness.

In the habitual tendency to identify with our particular activities and roles, we gradually become dependent on the results of these two things. We can also let the determinations of others affect our peace of mind, our sleep, happiness and contentment. The desire to please, the wish to be accepted, the determination to gain prestige, to get what we want, can dominate our consciousness. We think our survival or security depends totally on the acknowledgement of others. Not getting what we want, or losing what we have, throws us back on ourselves. If we do not fall back upon wisdom and clarity, then the pit of anxiety and fear beckons.

Mr Jones worked as an office manager in a multinational firm. One day at work he received a call telling him that his house was on fire. The caller said the firemen were struggling to keep the blaze under control. 'My home, my possessions, my books!' he cried. With lightning speed, he raced downstairs, charged with the terror of losing what he had. The receptionist yelled to him to stop but he took no notice as he ran through the revolving doors to the car park below. He had one thought in his mind – the desire to get home as quickly as possible. He drove recklessly through the streets towards his house. And then the receptionist called him on his mobile phone. 'I'm sorry, Mr Jones, there's been a mistake. Your house is not on fire. It's the house on the opposite side of the street.' 'Thank God,' he replied. Fear of losing what he had, total identification with his possessions, had made Mr Jones drive like a madman. He did not possess those items, they possessed him.

When we experience some level of disatisfaction it may be low-level unrest or it may be a general sense that something is wrong with the way things are. We suffer through fear, selfish desire and anger. Suffering over not getting what we want and suffering over losing what we have can become primary features of our existence. We then define these states of mind as side effects of living in the real world.

The Buddha makes it absolutely clear that the veil of suffering can dissolve, that we can pierce through the dramas of personal existence. We do not have to trap ourselves in the loop of struggle and recovery. Clinging, attachment and identification with changing conditions sow the seeds for suffering. In the mess of desires and projections, we block off our capacity to recognise the forces pushing and pulling our mind around. We may not even be aware of the processes that are operating within and without. It then becomes our lot to experience varying degrees of pleasure and pain broken by bouts of ordinariness in between.

When we are aware of ourselves and the conditions around us, we are able to see and work with every manifestation of suffering. In this respect, awareness is a key to the resolution of suffering. Awareness is the element which reveals inner and outer circumstances and thus is the starting point for change. Many people initially connect with the Dharma due to their awareness of the arising of suffering, gross or subtle, inward or outward. Some wish to develop a comprehensive and wise approach to their lives. Others wish to find practical signposts to realisation, or may be happy and successful in their respective fields of activity but do not delude themselves into thinking that they have reached genuine fulfilment. The Dharma points to the end of becoming, the completion of the evolutionary process, to Nirvana. It is no small claim.

In Pali the word for happiness is *sukkha*. What is considered *sukkha* for some people others consider *dukkha*. Some consider accumulation and attachment to property, wealth and position as *sukkha*, but the Dharma practitioner considers personal selfishness as *dukkha*. Mindful living becomes an invaluable tool for freeing our life from *dukkha*. The ability to work with suffering and dissatisfaction shows true development of mind. To make this possible we explore through experience each link of the Noble Eightfold Path in our lives. We have the opportunity in this life to discover the Unborn, Unmade, Undecaying. There is nothing else to compare.

INQUIRY

1. Ask yourself, 'What do I want? Is it worthwhile? Is it charged with fantasy? Is there an ethic underpinning what I want?'

2. Visualise not getting what you want. Could that even be preferable?

3. Ask yourself, 'What material thing(s) would I most hate to lose? What do I need to understand so as not to lose peace of mind as well?'

4. How do you experience the difference between those natural unpleasant feelings arising over the loss and separation, and indulgence in self-pity and despair?

5. Notice the difference in quality between clinging to an object, person or situation and connection without clinging.

Desire – A Cause of Suffering

One of the world's most powerful forces is desire. It has become a governing factor of existence. We live in a society that blatantly exploits desire through indoctrination, including the intense promotion of profit, consumer goods, careers and the determination to satisfy every whim.

In the desire to dominate or suppress, governments send armies and secret units to terrorise those they oppose. Terrorist organisations react likewise. It is the force of desire at work – to have, to get rid of, to deny, to retain.

Weapons used under the grip of desire obviously cause harm and terrible suffering to men, women, children and the environment. Every group has the desire to protect its vested interests, even if letting go or renouncing them might be for the common good. We cherish, cling to, and identify with our desires regardless of the impact of them on our lives, on others and on the earth itself.

We unconsciously identify with thoughts, intentions and results that combine to form the thrust of desire. This produces our ego at the expense of clarity and wisdom.

There are desires having no better aim than to satisfy the ego or perpetuate addictions. This may show itself in the obsessive pursuit of a particular objective. Numerous fantasies get charged with desire, breeding like mosquitoes in a swamp of dissatisfaction. There is the desire to be somebody special, to impress the fickle minds of others, to get rich or to move in the circles of the influential. There is no end to this cycle of wanting, wanting, wanting.

We have become gripped with desire, tormented and stuck in it. And, tragically, we nurture desire to try to get what we want from life. It is no wonder that death has become such a terrifying thought. Death makes a mockery of desire by severing every whim. No wonder the Buddha focused on desire as a major cause of suffering.

We are so preoccupied with desires that we cannot imagine a life without them. Life without desire seems to be unreal, abstract and unintelligible. But it's important we understand the expression of desire as a blind force, no matter how clever we think we are. We get glued to pursuing action and results. Self clings on to having and not having, being and not being. Success and failure then become uppermost in our mind, having an impact on our perceptions, feelings, thoughts and consciousness.

Ann was thirty-seven years old. She had been in a relationship for eight years but her partner did not want to start a family so she ended the relationship. She wanted a baby – desperately. As her desire grew stronger, she became more anxious about the possibility. In the supermarket, she felt jealous of mothers with babies and young children. Every time she met a new man, she wondered whether he would become the father of her child. She hated birthdays: they meant time was passing. It seemed that the fusion of biological impulses and personal desire now tormented her.

The Buddha showed the way to dissolve this insistent and often painful force of desire, whether gross or subtle. He pointed to wisdom and a clear way to be in touch with the here and now rather than in the shadow of painful desires. It is possible to realise a desireless life. All manifestations of desire are unacceptable from an enlightened standpoint. Such uncompromising statements can bring concern, if not confusion, for thoughtful people. For Ann, it meant accepting the reality of the situation and nourishing other areas of her life. She began to understand that life is not made to conform to personal desires.

Desire is single and its manifestations are many. *Don't we need a desire to go and brush our teeth? Don't we need a desire to read this book? Don't we need a desire to work towards enlightenment?* Obviously, we may need to use the language of desire to describe the movement of body, speech and mind. In Dharma language this movement becomes desire only when infected with ego, attachment and holding. This generates suffering in various forms. Aspiration, clear purpose, movement, wishes, wise action, and right effort express understanding, not 'desire'. It is important to make this distinction to understand the Second Noble Truth.

The teachings point to freedom from the *corruptive* influences of desire that taint our life, not to passive existence. We want to be with somebody one day and we want to get away from them the next. There is nothing fixed about desire. Any desire can become the primary reason for our existence. Without wisdom, we can collapse emotionally and physically under the weight of our desires.

Those who take on board too much, even for the best of reasons, engage in service neither for themselves nor others. Stress and anxiety are a common outcome affecting ourselves and others. We share the illusion that peace lies at the end of what we want. We study, create or work hard towards a particular end. Craving for particular results fills our consciousness. We tell ourselves that when we get to the end of the particular desire we shall finally experience peace. That is not peace.

True inner peace belongs to a different dimension of understanding altogether. What we experience at the end of the desire is relief from it. The authentic end of desire comes through the dissolution of the ego. Relief from desire is temporary.

Wisdom is the antidote to desire. It is the presence of wisdom that makes the difference. Without it, we spur our mind on in self-deluding ways, and we still say, 'That's our choice.' If so, then obviously such logic says we should choose to live free from suffering, be full of joy and welcome everything that happens to us.

It takes a lot more than claims of personal choice to find wisdom, to end suffering. It takes a profound inquiry and sustainable interest in the range of conditions that shape our lives. It would be a pity to wait for a huge personal drama to shake us out of our lethargy.

The end of desire signals the end of ego existence. In seeing through the phoney world of desire, we discover a way of being that is engaged, fulfilled and enlightened.

INQUIRY

1. *Notice the difference between right effort and becoming caught up in a desire that leads to problems.*

2. *Attend to the presence of I and my under the influence of desire.*

3. *Is there dependency on results for peace of mind?*

4. *What is the experience of not demanding anything from yourself or this world?*

6. *What is that which is neither influenced by right effort, nor desires?*

Liberation from Suffering

The Third Noble Truth is the consummation of the teachings. It means:

Seeing the Emptiness of self-existence, including all states of mind.
Discovering the Unborn, the Deathless, as the release from the made and the formed.
Cessation of karma, (unsatisfactory influences from the past).
Timeless discovery of non-dual wisdom.
Living an enlightened life.
Liberating insights into the nature of dependent arising.
Joy of Nirvana.

One would be hard pressed to find anywhere the Buddha proclaiming a peaceful state of mind as the fulfilment of the practice. Realisation of liberation from all manner of suffering, anguish and dissatisfaction may seem inconceivable to the ordinary, everyday mind unexposed to the Dharma. That does not put it out of reach. Even those who practise the Dharma may harbour the view that the task lies beyond human capacity. It is not unusual for profound teachings to get watered down to popularise them. There are a few sins in teaching the Dharma and one of them must surely be reducing the teachings to the overcoming of stress. A life totally dedicated to the Dharma embraces more than meditation and mindful exercises for coping calmly with daily life. While appreciating calmness and clarity of mind – features of the last two links of the Noble Eightfold Path – they can never serve as a substitute for liberation.

The Third Noble Truth speaks of an authentically enlightened existence, not a cool response to it. We should never forget that discovering a truly liberated life is much harder than we think. In these teachings, those who have realised liberation are called Noble Ones. They have found the way out of problematic existence. They have not generated a new construction but simply have ceased believing in and giving substance to the modes of the constructed self and its various standpoints. They have realised liberation. This is Nirvana. It is unformed, unmade, and not dependent on conditions for its presence. The realised ones know liberation as the way out of the jungle of discontent and lack of fulfilment. Nirvana does not belong to an unconscious state arising in meditation that fluctuates. Nor is it a condition of absolute detachment from the world or a state of annihilation.

In essence, liberation is the realisation of the end of suffering, the full emancipation of the human spirit and the joyful understanding of the nature of things. Cessation of suffering removes the struggle born of greed, hate and self-delusion. It eradicates that compelling need to pursue or gain things as an ultimately satisfying way of life. The emptiness of the ego, of any substance to *I* and *my*, is obvious.

Dharma teachings encourage us to resolve the force of wanting, to extinguish the problems, confusions and conflicts associated with it. This reveals the completion of the Path to Enlightenment. The cessation of dissatisfaction around wanting and not wanting points to the essence of the Third Noble Truth. This might seem an impossible undertaking. We think that our mind expresses only wanting or not wanting, and every action would appear to confirm this expression. All this is true for ordinary mind with ordinary consciousness but it cannot be said that this is how it is for everybody. We are then closing the door to enlightenment, preferring to take shelter within our fixed views.

Nirvana is knowing an emancipated life; it is not merely a clarity of mind. There is a danger that in making Nirvana into clarity of mind we substitute the unconditioned, unborn, unmade for the conditioned, born and made. All states of mind, pleasant and unpleasant, shallow and deep, calm or confused, arise owing to the presence of causes and conditions for them to arise. We use our perceptions and experiences to fix cause and effect. We live in a world that assumes the relationship and impact of things and events upon each other, and the truth of our perceptions. It is not through piling one effort on to another, nor through acts of will, that our natural freedom shines through.

The Noble Ones know that this remarkable liberation shines through states of mind – without dependency upon them. Knowing this releases much joy for the Noble Ones and also releases much love for others caught up in states of mind. This liberating discovery takes the grip of events out of one's life – not through detachment but through clarity, insight and an incomprehensible intimacy. The grip of the perception that we were born and that we die also loses substantiality. The relevance of birth and death only has real significance for those who identify the activities of *I* and *my* with mind and body.

In enlightenment there is no notion of wandering from one thing to another; there is nothing for the self to gain or achieve. There is no further evolution for the self, and desire and becoming have lost all relevance. Liberated people neither cherish self-existence nor withdraw from it; neither cling to others, nor reject them. They have done what has to be done. They have reached the top of the mountain that was always there in front of them. They know that the path is not the condition for the mountain. The mountain, that is the nature of things, stands firm and steady whether there is a path to it or not.

The 'world's' interactions with our 'perceptions' deceive us into thinking we live in touch with reality. We invest substance and reality in our perceptions even though our experience of the world keeps changing. It is these changing experiences and views that naturally refute any standpoint that the mind makes. We assume that we are an agent who acts upon the world and a recipient of other people's actions, who also act as agents. Infatuated with this way of thinking, we can't see a way out of it. It seems as though we keep switching our identities. One minute we are the agent, next minute others are. We live in a kind of bubble that produces suffering and dissatisfaction. The final delusion is believing that this is the way things really are. Morality, depths of meditation and wisdom shake out of us the complacency of such a view. They open out our whole field of awareness. The constructions of the self collapse. Everything is in place without beginning, middle or end. Wanting and not wanting, existence and non-existence produce a distorted world upon which all anguish comes to rely. There is nothing to grasp, nor possess, nor cling to. An enlightened life breaks us out of the spell of self-deception.

We are free. Utterly free.

The Path

In a world where suffering belongs to the everyday fabric of existence, it is peculiar to pay so much attention to the path which ends suffering. It seems like a distraction from getting on with our life. We might ask, 'Who would want to be involved in ending suffering since it seems an impossible undertaking?'

From one perspective, this is already the main priority of people's lives. Politicians tell us to study and work harder in order to increase our standard of living. Religion tells us we are sinners or have karma to work out. Psychologists tell us that our childhood conditions our lives. Society says we are not good enough until we have achieved a significant position and income.

If you give attention to your daily priorities, you will notice how much effort goes into the pursuit of making things better or easier. We want to overcome what we don't like and only taste what we like. These are strong forces at work. As a result of all these influences, we find ourselves driven on from one thing to another. Yet nobody ever came to the end of their life wishing they had spent more time in the office.

Karen worked for the world's largest software company. Along with the other staff, she had become a millionaire in a handful of years. She owned a very large, expensive house where she lived alone. Every year she bought herself a brand new Mercedes Benz. That was her life. There was no other life. She couldn't even think that there might be another way of life. Her colleagues wondered if she was a loyal servant to the company or a slave to the global ambitions of its owner. Gaining financial rewards and status bear little relationship to ending inner anguish. We need to be very, very clear about this.

It is no easy task to take an honest look at our life. We tend to think that if we have more possessions, money, status and influence, we are getting on well with our life. Perhaps we succeed, but even if we experience financial security it doesn't guarantee emotional security, adventure or the ability to enjoy ourselves. We go on working and working even when there is no real need to and when there is no excitement whatsoever left in the product. We don't know anything else. We live in a straitjacket, even if it's made of the best material.

If there is a mild yearning for change, we may have to cultivate contact with those people whose lives we truly admire. We may need to take small, tenuous steps to break out of the monotony of a daily routine that controls our existence. We may need to find every drop of inspiration possible. Visionary people inspired by love are willing to live in a state of financial insecurity to uphold a higher deal. It is hard to se the merit in spending a life in pursuit of financial security when death takes it all away.

If you examine your life you might need to ask about your relationship to your primary activities.

INQUIRY

1. *What really matters?*

2. *Do you have vision, passion, interest and skill?*

3. *What is the motive for your primary activities?*

4. *What challenges your heart as much as your mind?*

5. *Do you do things because you don't know what else to do?*

6. *Do you do things to get them over and done with?*

7. *Do you get burnt out?*

If we are going to find our way in life, it will mean finding a realignment with what matters. We may have to go away or take frequent long walks in order to take an honest look at our life. It will take time to dwell upon what matters and what doesn't matter. It may mean learning to take the slings and shots of outraged family and friends if we launch initiatives to express something noble and decent in our life. If we accept the challenge to find the way to a free and enlightened life, it may mean an enormous upheaval, a new birth. A major change from within may bring us much closer to our loved ones, to others in need, or it may put us on a solitary path to transformation.

Out of authentic change, there are three features which become indispensable: morality, awareness and wisdom. They are sure signals of a transformed life. Working together with these will enable us to stand steady in the face of misunderstanding or even virulent opposition. When we look at our involvements we may not see a way out. There *is* a way out. If we really listen to life, inner and outer, we will see what it is and we will have the strength of mind to follow the way. To enlighten our life means taking out the suffering or unsatisfying factors. It may mean that in the short term more suffering arises as we struggle to find our way. But there is the potential for discovering a liberating joy, not dampening down the spirit, not knuckling down to conform to others' demands. It may mean a change of role or outlook, or both.

On a retreat in the USA I remember giving a talk about the importance of integrity and moderation in lifestyle. I paraphrased Jesus of Nazareth: 'It's easier for a Cadillac to get through the keyhole of a door than for those who pursue wealth to reach the end of suffering.' I also quipped, 'Cadillacs and Porsches are probably symbols of inner poverty.' Right after the talk a friend whispered to me, 'Christopher, you live on donations. You may not know this but there is a Cadillac and a Porsche parked right next to each other in the centre's car park. Your donations for this retreat probably just went down by half!' I replied that I believe that the pursuit of wealth needs to be frequently challenged.

Contemporary religious authorities, gurus and spiritual leaders frequently avoid such censure of their devotees in case they lose their loyalty and their financial offerings. Not suprisingly, religious leaders, who claim renunciation, often like to associate themselves with the wealthy. Religion has no major relevance for the teachings of the Noble Eightfold Path. It might even act as a distraction. At its best, it reminds us of the deep things in life, but life ought to do that already.

We begin to fulfil our remarkable potential for full enlightenment when we investigate every area of our life. We start to take a genuine interest in the way our inner life influences circumstances. Observing the movements of our mind, we wake up to the value of a warm heart, clear mind and purposeful action. Daily life then reflects our commitment to enlightenment. All experiences become grist for the mill.

The teachings stress the importance of the Middle Way between two extremes. One is self-infatuation and the other is self-hate. They relate to each other, often finding themselves in mutual struggle. The practice of the Middle Way means we genuinely explore every feature of the Noble Eightfold Path. Our commitment serves as a reference point for all our priorities. We become willing to go through heaven and hell to remain true to the Path, no matter how much sacrifice it demands from us. Yet to keep true to the Middle Way we watch for any sign of clinging to it. We work with self-infatuation and self-blame, self-righteousness and self-condemnation. We follow the direct way to liberation, but we never forget the Path is only a metaphor.

I asked one person why he came on retreat He said: 'I love listening to the teachings. I love silence and meditating in the company of like-minded people.' For many the intensive retreat serves as a major point of awakening. The first awakening to the Path starts the extraordinary movement into the true way of things.

INQUIRY

1. *Are you on the Path to Enlightenment?*
2. *If so, what are the signs?*
3. *What ways can your path be further developed?*
4. *If not on the Path, why not?*
5. *Do you have impressions of yourself or others that inhibit inquiry into the experience of living?*
6. *Are you awake or living in a dream?*

THE NOBLE
EIGHTFOLD PATH

Let one purpose confess to move our hearts,
That is to expand this vista of life,
To shake off the hold of conformity,
So insights thrust their way through this mind.

Introduction

The Noble Eightfold Path consists of:

1. Right Understanding.
2. Right Intention.
3. Right Speech.
4. Right Action.
5. Right Livelihood.
6. Right Effort.
7. Right Mindfulness.
8. Right *Samadhi.*

The Noble Eightfold Path serves as the greatest challenge to our life. It demands that we leave no stone unturned. There is nothing whatsoever that we can think, say or do that does not bear a direct relationship to the Eightfold Path. The links remind us to pay attention to every feature of our life. The word *right* indicates skilful rather than imploring us to take up a moralistic attitude to each of the links. There is no point in taking up the Eightfold Path if it contributes to divisiveness – if we identify with those on the Path and condemn those not on the Path.

Through a cursory glance at the Noble Eightfold Path, we might think that we are living in full accordance with each factor. If that is true, then it means we are living an enlightened life, free from selfishness, aggression and any confusion. If we know in our hearts that we have work to do on ourselves, then we begin exploring all the links. Forgetting the cursory glance, we focus our minds wholeheartedly to see what we must develop and what we must overcome.

As our commitment to the Path of Enlightenment gets stronger, we will know that we are walking the Path. It will not be a matter of fitting the Path into our life but rather our life fitting into the Path. We will come to understand the nature of things. We will love access to the depths of experiences and the range of insights. In walking the Path to Enlightenment, we honour ourselves and honour life itself. There is nothing more important. Do not delay.

Right Understanding

Right understanding comes in two ways. First, we develop the capacity to witness problems, explore ways to work with them and gain insights that make a difference. We cultivate all the remaining seven links as a contribution to right understanding. As we develop our understanding, problems begin to recede. We bring greater awareness to the issues of life. We take notice of the subtle levels of dissatisfaction and unrest. We find a greater appreciation for happiness, love and peace of mind. We begin to understand the way our activities contribute to a depth of presence and insight. We see also the way we harm ourselves and others. There is a growing capacity for change.

The second way is equally important and serves as a balance to the first. It is the understanding of the importance of silence and solitude. In solitude, we reduce significantly the level of input on the sense doors. We find time to put aside all that makes up our daily life at home. We forget the problems of our life and this earth to renew our relationship with ourselves and with the moment. In solitude, we understand what it means to stop making demands upon ourselves and others. We let go of the demands that organisations, society and family make upon us. We listen to ourselves. We explore the difficult and cultivate what is noble.

It's wonderful to be able to understand the nature of life in a fresh way. It requires a passion and love for life to see each day as something fresh rather than a monotonous continuity of the old. When we experience that intimacy with each day, our mind hardly ever needs to dwell on past or future. There may be one or two things we need to remember or some attention we need to give to some plans for the future. But we know they take suprisingly little time. Daily life absorbs us into itself. We belong to it, exuding happiness and contentment from our being. Getting absorbed into our soap operas is no substitute for experiencing our connection with our life on this earth.

Global thinking, holistic values and the awareness of interdependency express a way of understanding that contributes to wisdom. It is not enough, of course, to participate in thoughtful approaches to existence. We can write papers on the importance of global awareness. But the depth of unity of understanding comes from a profound awareness, insightful meditations, and a day-to-day commitment.

One of the most intense gaps that appears in consciousness can occur in the inflamed perception of *you* and *me*. If ever there was an area that requires understanding this surely is it. The *you* and *me* become a priority, setting perceptions, feelings and memories against each other. The duality then looms larger and larger in life. Clearly, there's something unhealthy about this. We enter into endless complications with all the effort to find a resolution. We peer at each other through pictures and images.

It's hardly surprising that we cannot see the other person clearly. We only see our state of mind. We have put so many layers on to the picture of that person that the person becomes obscured. We distort that person like those amusing mirrors at the fairground. Unfortunately the distortions in our minds are no joke. We are all linked through a common existence. This experience and insight shows something remarkable and authentic occurring in consciousness. We might say that in simple terms separation reveals lack of understanding by producing the appearance of a divided reality. Right understanding ends that division.

Each time we believe in one self pitted against another self, we hide the deeper reality of the situation. We lack insight into the nature of things. So if we turn our attention to what gives rise to fragmentation and ensuing conflicts, we move towards right understanding and away from misunderstanding. It is an enormous task. We should never underestimate its significance. It will have an impact on every area of our life. Our values, personal, interpersonal, social and political, will undergo a profound shift.

It's not unusual for people in conflict to be united in their negativities when engrossed in bitter strife with a lover, family member, friend or neighbour. As we develop a sense of right understanding, we open up new ways to examine a situation. We won't live reactively or drift along. We will recognise the practical importance of the various aspects of the Noble Eightfold Path. We simply stop, inquire into our lives and become aware of our immediate world. That's where the inspirations ought to be.

We reflect our view of self and the world. We imagine that the self resides inside the body – one with it, outside the body, or both. We think the world exists outside the self, inside it, both, or neither. Our experience of self and other varies considerably. One minute we may be thinking everything is in our mind, the next minute thinking everything that matters is outside our mind. We get so convinced about both ways of thinking that we completely forget how one refutes the ultimate authority of the other.

PRACTICE

1. *See the present moment for itself, not as an effect of the past or a cause of the future.*

2. *In times of well-being, drop everything and let that sense naturally deepen.*

3. *Notice as many changes as possible in a day to contribute to overcoming clinging.*

The self and the world, me and you, are ways of viewing. If we are willing to go deeply into all of this, we won't get knocked off balance through living in a legacy of misperceptions. There is a way of understanding that is sublime. We realise that the view that arises is simply that. We do not have to carry it around like a weapon. It's as though we have been living in darkness and come across a lamp that reveals the splendour of things. Awareness is that lamp.

There is a right understanding that stands free from a fixed or changeable view of the world. This understanding shows us non-clinging to standpoints. It ends suffering and dissatisfaction born of misperception, formations of self, and clinging. The inner life often works like a potter's wheel that makes all sorts of formations and views. We believe what it generates and creates simply as that. We don't deceive ourselves into thinking that what the mind creates reveals the way things truly are.

We also need to understand the nature of a life dedicated to Dharma teachings and practices. We may love the Dharma's common-sense approach. It points to our enlightenment and provides the resources to make that possible. We may take a short- or long-term view.

1. Some conclude that it means, 'Practise, practise, practise meditation to reach liberation.'
2. Some believe, 'Liberation lies in the hands of a tiny group of spiritual masters.'

These people imagine that one word, one glance or laying the hands upon the head by a spiritual master is enough. Some may have been profoundly touched by such an experience, but they still have to do the washing-up. Having had such an experience, they may dispense with practice, association with the wise, and meditative inquiry into existence. Time goes by. This wonderful experience at the hands of the master fades. Suffering arises. Doubts arise. Perhaps the master did not have the power to transform to any depth. Perhaps the ego is stronger than the penetrative stare of the guru.

True teachings and practices point to a liberation here and now resolving once and for all the problems of life. If we cling to practice, it also becomes a problem, as if we didn't have enough already. It then becomes an obstruction to discovering an unparalleled freedom. We develop our practice for right understanding of an enlightened life. In liberation we realise there is nothing whatsoever worth clinging to. The master and the method have that in common.

INQUIRY

1. *What do you really need to understand?*
2. *In Dharma language to understand means to be clear about and at peace with. Intellectual understanding is not a real understanding. What will bridge the gap?*
3. *What do you need to be clear about to understand someone with whom you have a problem?*
4. *We cannot organise and control life. It refuses to conform to our demands. Is there something profound you need to understand about this?*
5. *What is your relationship to spiritual practice and spiritual masters?*

Right Intention

This second link in the Noble Eightfold Path embraces two important features of the mind, intention and attitude. Both influence and support each other. Knowing ourselves includes attending regularly to these expressions of our inner life. At times, we notice that our intention and attitude are wholesome, which contributes to greater happiness and peace of mind. At other times we notice our intention and attitude are unwholesome, which contributes to negativity and dissatisfaction within. We can become our own best friend or our own worst enemy.

Right intention flowers from awareness of interconnection and as a result of the dissolution of an unwise attitude. It means that we regularly examine our motives for what we do, and develop ways to change our behaviour. We listen to the feedback of others. Right intention reflects an understanding of the dependent arising nature of circumstances (that nothing can arise without suitable conditions for its arising) and the way events co-operate for something to happen. Understanding Dependent Arising is a very important aspect of the Buddha's teachings.

We often notice the importance of attitude. We can listen to others far more easily if we appreciate their intention. It is harder for us to listen to their words and tone of voice if we mistrust or dislike their approach. *You have an attitude* has become common parlance. Such one-liners rarely make a difference to a person who pushes their views down our throat.

At times we adopt an aggressive and demanding attitude. We then pull others into our web of standpoints. We get very high-minded about things that we believe really matter. This often has the impact of irritating people or making them suspicious about our objectivity. We pressure them to agree with us, try to get them upset or make them as negative as we are. Our information might be correct but the intention is unhealthy and unhelpful. We may have the attitude that everybody else is at fault except ourselves. The world is not made to fit in with everything we want. Others have their life to lead. They are not going to be at our disposal all the time. We have to make that very clear inside ourselves.

When we hold to a fixed position we get out of touch with each other. We may have the desire to embarrass, harm or humiliate. Getting our own way matters more than the facts, but people are not stupid; they often recognise our real intentions. All manner of suffering between people arises from unwise intentions acknowledged or denied.

In the depths of difficulties, our intention to get out of a painful condition may not be enough. We usually need the co-operation of others. I was leading twenty days of intensive retreat in Bodh Gaya, India, at a monastery five minutes' walk from the tree where the Buddha was enlightened. One night a young Western woman fell down a well in a corner of the monastery. We heard her crying for help. In order for her to get out of the well, three things needed to happen. There had to be the rope as the means. People standing at the top of the well had to take the strain. She had to have the intention to take hold of the rope. We pulled her out – wet, embarrassed but not hurt.

It can be a significant practice to dedicate ourselves to watching our intention. As we become more proficient we may notice a diminishing in the compelling forces of wanting, harming or any predilection towards acts of cruelty. To change such conditioning marks an evolutionary step for a human being. We would think differently about people and things. We would not hide behind crude generalities, explosive rhetoric or tiresome views – obviously, none of that supports a sensitive awareness. Inner change points us in the right direction towards a life not conditioned by various factors that shape unsatisfactory intentions of mind.

INQUIRY

1. Do you have a questionable intention towards a situation?

2. Examine the attitude and its consequences.

3. Name it and develop an alternative.

4. Apply the resolution even if initially it feels abstract and unreal.

At times, we refuse to acknowledge that our attitude is unhealthy. Joe had decided to join the staff of a respected retreat centre. He thought the atmosphere of silence and peace, and the opportunity to serve others, would be beneficial. He soon found out that service demanded a great deal of time, focus and energy. Joe became increasingly resentful. He attended fewer and fewer staff meetings. He became a minimalist. He complained to anybody who would listen that the staff were not getting enough support. When he left he said he was burnt out. His parting shot was: 'Being here did nothing for me.' We cannot grow as a human being when our mind is fixed in such a way. We become our own worst enemy.

The inner life with its conflicting intentions is an extraordinary thing. A healthy intention can give way to an unhealthy intention within the same person. We say time heals. It may be that the conditions for disappointment and resentment simply fade until a similar situation happens next time. When our thoughts and words keep finding fault we remain caught up in negativity. It takes practice, skill and insight to sustain a healthy attitude towards the events of life.

Many plays, songs and films explore these long-standing issues of people's struggle with each other. Love, pain and struggle are common themes in popular culture. Films frequently offer the viewing public a major deception. The end of the film invariably shows the triumph of good over evil, right over wrong, success over failure.

The only problem is that life simply doesn't follow such a simplistic world-view. It is a challenge to face the world of conditions and their results. We might desperately want things to work out for the best. Wanting is one thing, outcome may be something else.

Joseph and Martha had been together for several years but had drifted apart due to their mutual need for greater independence. Their children ensured that there would be a continuity of connection for many years to come. Not going out to work, Martha took possession of the children and acted as though she was the primary parent. She never took into account that her ex-husband worked many hours every week to support her and the children. She confined his access to the children to one weekend a month.

Ideally Joseph wanted to have more time with his children. His ex-wife would have none of that. Saturday morning, 10 a.m. sharp was the time for collection. Sunday evening, 6 p.m. sharp was the time to return the children. He loved the children and Martha's attitude hurt. He knew that she used her control over the children to hurt him. It could be due to disappointment with her life, a wish for revenge, or jealousy over his new girlfriend. He didn't know. Years went by. The children grew up, but by then it was too late. He found it hard to forgive her. He remained as stuck in his attitude as she was in hers.

INQUIRY

1. *Are you willing to change an unhealthy intention?*
2. *Are you constantly out to get what you want and not considering others?*
3. *Do you ever intend to hurt or harm others?*
4. *What shows a healthy attitude negating an unhealthy one?*
5. *Do you maintain a firm intention to enlighten every area of your life?*
6. *Are there intentions in an enlightened life?*

Right Speech

When I was a Buddhist monk in Thailand, my mother came to visit me. We were walking together in the Monastery of the Reclining

Buddha in Bangkok. It is a place popular with foreign tourists wishing to see the eighty-foot-long statue. An evangelical missionary from Georgia, USA, approached me and asked me what I was doing dressed up as a Buddhist monk. After I explained to him, he said, 'The Lord Jesus came into my life and saved me. I was an alcoholic and my marriage was on the rocks. Jesus can do the same for you.'

I expressed appreciation. I spoke of the importance of religion to heal. I said that in my monastery alcoholics, addicts and terrorists were also saved through the Buddha's teachings and meditation. He said: 'I don't believe you, boy. Only Jesus saves. You're the son of Satan.' I laughed. I turned to my mother, a practising Roman Catholic, and said: 'If I'm the son of Satan, who does that make you?' It seemed to me that the missionary hadn't heard of right speech.

Practising Buddhists receive training in right speech. There are generations of teachings about the way language impacts on life. One learns about unskilful speech and its impact, and the benefits of skilful speech. We use language to give shape to our everyday world. What we say influences the minds of others, near and far. Our sophisticated language distinguishes us from other species.

Reluctant to appear negative, Buddhists have often suppressed their critical voice. In their wish to appear kind, tolerant and thoughtful, they have often adopted a passive attitude to situations rather than speaking their mind in skilful ways. Their tolerance has invited intolerance, their passivity has invited hatred. This has had widespread consequences in Buddhist countries. When asked why terrible tragedies and obscene regimes have ruled Buddhist countries, Buddhists will often say, 'Karma', and overlook the various causes.

Right speech requires clarity of mind and freedom from confusion about the meaning of non-duality, that super-ordinary reality embracing self and other. Buddhists often feel that to criticise firmly and harshly means being dualist. An increasing number of Western Buddhists have adopted the same polite, diplomatic tone. But dualism refers to greed, anger and delusion, not to critical analysis to end greed, anger and delusion.

We must feel free to voice our concern while being vigilant around anger, self-righteousness and moralising. There is too much anger in the world already; it does not need any more. Right speech is a difficult area of life. It requires mindfulness, practice and insight. Our speech reveals our attitudes and priorities as much as the subjects that we talk about. Language is a tool revealing simultaneously the inner and the outer.

There are certain things to bear in mind. Before we speak, our practice considers:

1. Right person – in distress we can go from one person to another looking for comfort. We get overwhelmed with contradictory advice or having to endure others relating their similar stories. If we avoid communication, we bottle up issues inside.

2. Right place – to communicate on deep matters requires a supportive and caring environment. People must feel safe. Due to familiarity and isolation, the home can be a dangerous place to resolve conflict. The raising of the voice is usually the first alarm signal.

3. Right time – we rarely resolve important matters when under pressures of time. Launching into a tirade with one's partner at midnight about the state of the relationship invites more suffering.

4. Right subject – we require some understanding of the listener(s) before we open our mouths. Dharma practice of right speech includes awareness of the area of common interest and the intention that accompanies it.

These guidelines help others but also ourselves. Without wisdom we might trigger conflict and confusion. This easily occurs when our will overrides any of the above considerations. Matters involving beliefs, health, emotions, money and the future can generate intolerable demands upon others and ourselves.

We explore what it means to speak that which is true and useful. We are also prone to idle talking, lies, backbiting, gossip – all forms of unwise speech. There is a certain kind of pleasure in these forms of speech that undermines respect for others. We often have a salacious appetite to know intimate details of the personal lives of others. It gives us the feeling of being in the know. We want to be in touch with the hidden goings-on in people's lives. But we may hardly be aware how cruel and hurtful it is to whisper behind the backs of others. It is better to preserve noble silence than enter into such forms of communication.

Particular tendencies operate, born of the combination of perceptions and feelings. Mental chatter gets verbalised, making gossip an announcement of our superficial state of mind. Some people become adept in secretly thinking one thing and saying another. They praise somebody publicly and privately plan to destroy them. But our so-called private world is very public. It doesn't require a special gift to be able to read the intentions of others.

Views and opinions enter into conversation often accompanied by various generalisations masquerading as truth. Such conversations expose the gross mind charged with deluded opinions and prejudice. Our speech wanders in and out of misleading ideas without any determination to put what we say into perspective. It is valuable to be wary of such concepts as 'never', 'only', 'always', 'every' and 'invariably'. These concepts blind us to the exceptions. Skilful conversation moves away from the general to the specific.

Given the opportunity, some people will speak about themselves incessantly. They seem to want to bore their way into our mind. The prevailing thought for the listener focuses inward on the strategy to stop the person, escape or change the subject. There is a limit to our endurance of hearing *I* and *my* from another. Others cling to their privacy, hating communication with others.

It is ennobling to work on speech. It uplifts the quality of our life, generates love for others and brings dignity to the field of communication. We have the ability to put ourselves into the situation of others. We have the capacity to understand others. We do not have to sink to the level of others. Let us apply awareness and effort to wise speech. It then becomes an important stepping stone to understanding the field of communication. We allow all language, wholesome and unwholesome, to rest in noble silence that is beyond words. The teachings point towards the influence of language, both wholesome and unwholesome, and that liberation which is beyond both.

INQUIRY

1. *Be mindful of the use of* I *and* my *in speech.*
2. *Are you afraid to express your concerns if you find yourself listening*

to gossip, backbiting and malicious comments about a third person?

3. *Practise expressing appreciation for another so that he or she has a genuine sense of their worth.*

4. *If what you have to say matters a great deal to yourself and other(s) then ask inwardly deeply beforehand, 'How can I handle this skilfully?' If possible, make time for quiet reflection on wise speech until heart and mind is steady and clear.*

5. *We perceive a difference between language and silence. Can both dissolve into each other?*

Right Action

Right action refers to every expression of body, speech and mind. Our activities tend to start in the mind and then find their expression in speech and body. We develop right action through awareness of all three of these areas in our lives. By addressing all three, we know the way of the mind and touch the depths of the heart. Simply stated, when we are involved with right action we cease to cause harm to others or ourselves through violence, abuse or exploitation. This is the practice of treating others and our world as we wish to be treated. It provides a personal, social, political and global ethic.

Once a year I fly to Israel to conduct a retreat for around one hundred and fifty Israelis. In that country, as elsewhere, there is a growing interest in the Dharma and the practices of tolerance, non-violence, awareness and depths of meditation.

A number of Israelis and I also travel to the West Bank where I facilitate a joint workshop with Palestinians. We meet on the top floor of a clinic in the town of Nablus. Many of our Palestinian hosts, who put us up in their homes, have served prison sentences. Many Israelis have served in the military. Every Israeli and Palestinian has experienced suffering as a result of their historical conflict. Nobody escapes. One Palestinian told me that he had been engaged in armed struggle against Israeli soldiers in southern Lebanon. He said, 'We could see the whites of their eyes as we fired our rifles. We were all young guys. Then suddenly I realised we could only resolve our differences through exchanging words, not bullets and mortars. That's why I am here at this meeting.'

The only solution for the Israelis and Palestinians is to free themselves from clinging to their identity as Israelis and Palestinians. They can then begin to find each other's common humanity. Then neither fear nor rage will colour their perceptions of each other. Trust comes through listening and through taking risks to know about the plight of others. Not to explore communication leaves us vulnerable to latent tendencies which can condemn or harm. When pressure and prejudice build up from within we become a danger to ourselves and others. To meet in order to resolve differences is a statement of right action.

Underlying or latent tendencies can wreck even the best intentions. The consequences of one foolish action can have reverberations for years. No matter how strong, the ripples remain finite, they do not go on for ever. The results of our actions may seem to outweigh the causes but that is due to our blindness to all the other factors involved. One small act of carelessness can launch devastating consequences. At times, life seems brutally unfair. However, life is neither fair nor unfair.

It had been a sudden impulse. The young man had no idea what got into him. He had been in the department store when he spotted a purse resting on the top of an old lady's bag. He snatched it and ran but before he got outside a member of staff grabbed him. The young man collapsed sobbing and pleading to be released, but the store had a policy of prosecuting all thieves. The police came. They informed his parents. His father and mother were angry and distressed. Because of this single moment of lack of wise attention, the young man and his family endured weeks of worry waiting to appear in the juvenile courts. Acting on impulse cost him dearly.

Our capacity to reflect on cause and effect can sober our minds to a remarkable degree. Right action emerges at times out of our ability to say *no*, to show restraint, to let go and to avoid; sometimes it might be necessary to grit our teeth and take long, deep breaths to protect our resolve. We might need the wisdom of others.

Greed, hate and delusion sow the seeds for unwise action, creating a hell for ourselves, if not others. The absence of these three forces enables generosity, kindness and clarity to express itself. If we concentrate our minds on tackling the greed, hate and delusion within, we will allow the wholesome expression of our inner life to manifest effortlessly. The root of the pure in our heart flowers naturally when not obscured by the dark shadow of the ego.

Some people learn from their mistakes either in the past or present and change their state, inwardly or outwardly, or both. Others refuse to change. They resist, no matter how much turmoil they create, but unless motivation to change arises from within them, there is nothing one can do but understand their imprisonment. The mental state of idleness and apathy incapacitates the individual, both psychologically and physically.

We have observed how much trouble we create for ourselves when we blindly comply with pressure. We feel hurt and used, we feel like a weakling. We hate ourselves for conforming to someone out of desire to be accepted or fear of rejection. Right action comes from clear intention and freedom from dependency on results. Fear influences action or prevents it.

INQUIRY

1. *Be aware of a manageable fear that arises.*

2. *Name it as fear and explore what you are afraid of.*

3. *Describe through reflection, in written form or to another, its limitation.*

4. *Practise taking steps to cut through the fear.*

Genuine right action carries with it a fearless attitude out of consideration for sentient beings. It is the soil in which understanding grows. Skilful action may spark off disputes, even in the most well-intentioned mind. Others view the results of what we do in a different way than we might view them ourselves. Interpretation of results rests in many minds, not just our own. In the last resort, we have to be honest with ourselves and live with the truth of our intentions, regardless of the praise or blame of others.

At times we might ask ourselves, 'Is this the right thing to do?' We can hear many voices from within — *yes, no, don't know, sooner* or *later*. We can hear similar voices too from without. They may be voices of authority, voices of experience, friends, family and strangers. Where can we turn for answers? In these teachings we can rely on the Dharma. Ethics – personal, social, environmental –

are criteria for what is right and wise. 'Who benefits?' we can ask ourselves; 'Am I placing integrity before prestige?'

Out of such reflection, right understanding can flower into right action. We will be grateful for our capacity to say *yes* or *no* or *don't know* to what is offered. The wise fish leave the bait of the fishermen alone.

INQUIRY

1. *What are the primary activities of your daily life? Is there stress in these activities? Are you ignoring the stress or addressing it?*

2. *If something needs to change in your activities, what is it?*

3. *Do the activities of your life genuinely include wholesome creativity, service and exposure to wisdom? Are these three areas fringe interests?*

4. *If you see your actions are unwholesome, due to habit and desire, are you finding people who can help point the way out of this trap?*

5. *Joy and happiness are a natural outcome of right action. Does your experience confirm this?*

6. *What is actionless action?*

Right Livelihood

As another link in the Noble Eightfold Path, right livelihood considers the relationship of the individual to the results of his or her work on people, animals and the environment. When involved in right livelihood our attitude and motivation matter. When work simply becomes the vehicle to enable more and more consumption, or when it supports degradation of the earth and its people, then it certainly becomes questionable.

Mindful of unemployment figures, politicians take the view that any work, no matter how soul-destroying, is better than no work at all. Right livelihood fulfils the aspirations of the individual and the genuine needs of the community. We need technology that supports the well-being of life, not the destruction of it. Right livelihood relates to community, both local and global, with local production for local needs. Regeneration, restoration and renewal embrace aspects of right livelihood. One of the aims of right livelihood is to make meaningful and satisfying work available to all. If we feel concern about the quality of life, then surely we want our work to contribute to the well-being of others, including ensuring that others receive the necessities of life such as wholesome food, clothing, a home and medicine. Such livelihood contributes to the uplifting of the body, mind and spirit of all. This makes it noble.

Work is a difficult issue for the thoughtful person to explore if he or she has an investment in a questionable livelihood. Such a person can hardly talk about their doubts at work since it might generate hostility and defensiveness from colleagues. People may not understand the depths of a dilemma about the value or significance of a particular job. There are no agencies of support to help employers or employees explore the depths of significance of right livelihood. You are left to get on with it, or get out.

The Dharma specifies various forms of unwholesome employment. These include producing and selling weapons, firearms, poison and harmful drugs; wilful destruction of life; exploitation of men, women and children; and promotion of violence and cruelty. I believe that any kind of involvement in work that deliberately causes harm to others and our environment is unacceptable, including promotion of cigarette smoking, boxing and animal experiments. I also believe that the exploitation of workers and customers to increase profits constitutes further expressions of unwholesome livelihood. Not surprisingly, those involved in forms of unacceptable occupation often condemn advocates of right livelihood for moralising.

There are some spiritual traditions, East and West, which would never question the manner of people's livelihood, claiming that the form of work has nothing to do with religious beliefs. We cannot get off that lightly in Dharma teachings. How we earn a living matters; it matters a great deal.

An international religious organisation promoting the use of mantra meditation took out a string of advertisements in the financial pages of serious daily newspapers. They advised readers to take up a mantra – for a price – to 'recharge their batteries'. The guru and his appointed teachers conveniently neglected the ethics of work in promoting their form of meditation. The value of the mantra gets corrupted when the daily meditator uses the extra energy to pursue certain ends selfishly and aggressively. Better they saved their money and did less work rather than buying the mantra. We need to look deeply into ourselves to see what is acceptable and what is not. We give much time to our mode of livelihood. This may mean a great upheaval in our life. It is vital that a person looks at his or her livelihood from a humanitarian and global standpoint.

INQUIRY

1. *Does everything take second place to money and career?*
2. *What shows ethics and integrity in your work?*
3. *Do you suppress your views when with colleagues?*
4. *Do you express concern for customers, clients, etc. as a daily priority?*

If you are unemployed:

1. *Are there expressions of creativity and service in your daily life?*
2. *Does your mind fall into cynicism or do you retain your dignity?*
3. *Is there the willingness to take initiatives and connect with others?*

Although it sounded grand for Richard to be a scientist, he knew otherwise. He worked in a science laboratory experimenting on animals for a major pharmaceutical company. There was no sense of awe and mystery in his work. He considered it mostly banal and monotonous rather than being on the edge of some breathtaking discovery. He knew his real concerns were for his peers to acknowledge him as a good scientist, to have job security and to put his children through private education.

He had never discussed with his colleagues the morality of their numerous experiments on animals. Occasionally, they ridiculed anti-vivisection organisations and that was as near as they came to talking about the issue. One day Richard got a shock. In a school debate, his son had argued strongly for alternative methods of research. Dismayed, the scientist asked his son whether he was ashamed of his father's profession. The son said, 'Yes', and had told the class exactly that during the debate.

This forced Richard to face himself. The claim of scientific objectivity lost its relevance compared to what his son thought of him. He realised that so-called objectivity relates directly or indirectly to human experience and priorities. Ultimately, he could not separate his career from intentions, values and relationships and quit the laboratory. His son was thrilled.

I would also include forms of questionable livelihood such as becoming a gambler, speculator, or promoter of deceptive information; and profiteering by exploiting others. These activities show obsession with gain at the expense of peace of mind for oneself and others. The pursuit of a career to elevate the self hardly ranks as a noble way of life. To pursue work to elevate the self is a waste of our existence.

There are livelihoods which deserve an honest self-examination as well, such as working in factory farms; some kinds of advertising; various forms of entertainment, such as striptease and crude humour; selling intoxicants and tobacco. These forms of work may not be classified as unwholesome, but we must not be afraid to question their impact on others, ourselves and other sentient beings. It is a matter of personal responsibility.

If we approach our daily lives in a responsible way it is less likely that ambitious and neurotic strivings will take over. With authority comes power. A clear signal of the excess of any position of authority occurs when the desire for it breeds in us intolerance, impatience and negativity towards others. The role becomes the outlet for unresolved arrogance and bullying. Others have to do as they are told. Such an attitude corrupts even the highest forms of livelihood.

One of the greatest joys in our life is when we can bring together love and labour. To have a passion for work knowing the far-reaching benefits is special. It is our birthright. It is to honour a noble way of life. To work free from desire for a substantial income lifts an enormous burden off our shoulders. Wisdom safeguards a noble role from becoming corrupted. Right livelihood serves as a powerful cornerstone for social change embracing both role and attitude. Ego is no substitute for a noble vision. To serve others is a reward in itself.

INQUIRY

1. *Is your work satisfying and fulfilling or deadening?*

2. *Would you be willing to be unemployed rather than engage in an unwholesome livelihood?*

3. *If you have disposable income, what happens to it?*

4. *Have you researched the companies who invest your money?*

5. *What ways do you show compassion to those less fortunate than yourself?*

Right Effort

When we were children we probably had it drummed into us that we had to make an effort and strive hard for success. We were told that we wouldn't get anywhere in life unless we did. Making such an effort placed us in competition with others and instilled in us the notion of being a *success* or being a *failure* with little understanding of the consequences of either. We put in effort at school, sports and work for the elevation of our self at the expense of other selves. We might have believed in the survival of the fittest, thus allowing its ideology to rule our lives. Or we might have noticed that intensity of competitiveness took the enjoyment and love out of activities, even breeding at times egotism and inner rage.

Few of us were given the opportunity to explore the valid application of right effort which works for the benefit of all. Right effort stands linked to other factors on the Noble Eightfold Path. At times, it takes a real determination to sustain right effort to walk the Path to Enlightenment. It takes effort to develop and maintain wise practice and effort to overcome and avoid whatever gets in the way of practice.

But isn't right effort a form of desire? Aren't we supposed to get rid of all desire? There is a distinction between desire and effort. It's a very important one. In Dharma language, desire means ego, selfishness, dependency on results, and is pervaded with the ignorance of consequences. Right effort reflects a noble aspiration to realise liberation. It comes from awareness to fulfill our human potential. Of course, our aspiration and effort for enlightenment can become corrupt through ego. When effort becomes desire we often become very judgemental, even cynical, of others with a similar aspiration or lack of it.

History is awash with religious figures and so-called saints who stopped the effort of looking into themselves. Eventually their egos ran riot. In Rishikesh, a sacred town of India in the foothills of the Himalayas, a yogi spent twelve years in a cave some miles upriver from the small town. When he returned he began judging all the renunciates, yogis and ashramites for not applying enough effort to gain *moksha* (liberation). Soon, the other renunciates who were striving for enlightenment avoided his presence and his menacing gaze. The yogi had spent all those years in a cave, only to emerge with an arrogant and conceited personality. What a waste of effort.

The Buddhist tradition points to the Noble Eightfold Path rather than to the behaviour of gurus as a reminder to explore every area of daily life. Right effort is one link in the path. The Buddha taught what he called the four Right Efforts. These four are to:

1. Develop the wholesome.
2. Maintain the wholesome.
3. Overcome the unwholesome.
4. Avoid the unwholesome.

1. At Gaia House in south Devon, we offer about thirty retreats a year, with teachings and practices for people interested in meditation, insight and knowing a liberated life. Some who come to us are dealing with major issues such as life-threatening illness, bereavement, the break up of a long relationship, or a deep sense of lack of self-worth. Feeling unsatisfied, some are developing thoughtful approaches to life. Others come for inner renewal or to awaken to enlightenment. They make the effort to enter and stay in an environment of meditation and inquiry. Some retreatants have to put a lot of effort into their practice. There is no other way for them. It's an effort to sit still in meditation several sessions a day, to walk mindfully and slowly in meditation. It's often an effort to stay steady in the here and now to witness this moment clearly. Their noble effort brings its own reward through clarity and realisation.

2. We then develop and maintain right effort in the face of life's circumstances. In this way the mind becomes open and expansive, able to see and accommodate situations. We maintain our practice through daily application in numerous circumstances. Not only will we benefit personally through maintaining generosity, kindness and clarity but others will benefit as well. It is worth making the effort for all of this.

3. Through out practice of developing and maintaining what is beneficial, and overcoming and avoiding what is not beneficial, we free ourselves from what was formerly overwhelming. Compelling mental states that influence addictive behaviour can be powerful forces to overcome in the mind. It requires vigilance, even willpower, to break through these habits. Inner and outer resources to overcome problems need to be cultivated.

4. Avoiding the unwholesome points to the capacity to steer our mind away from the forces of attraction and aversion that result in confusion, if not nightmares. We should never underestimate the potency of such inner forces and the mess they can make of our lives. It can look like escapism, yet restraint or letting go signals the mark of natural wisdom. At times, it is vital that we keep away from certain people and places if such encounters are likely to provoke harm to ourselves or others.

It is necessary, if not urgent, to make the effort to maintain our focus on enlightenment. We can connect with others who have first-hand experience of going deep into themselves. We learn from those who have transformed their lives or dissolved difficult mind-states. For example, what we do literally with our hands tells us a lot about our values, our state of mind and the course of our life. The practice of mindful use of our hands will contribute to the wisdom of restraint and wholesomeness of creative initiatives.

PRACTICE

1. *Sit in a meditative posture with eyes closed and direct attention to the hands*

2. *Experience the form of the hands, the sensations and temperature.*

3. *Reflect on the primary purposes for which you use your hands in daily life*

4. *Where is the creativity? What actions show kindness and compassion?*

5. *What are the habits? What provokes agitation?*

We like to think of ourselves as human beings but the sense of *being* often seems lacking. People and planet pay a price for this. For the most part, we have become human *busyings. Homo ignoramus* or *Homo shopiens* then replaces *Homo sapiens!* We hardly find time to stop and take a real look at our life. We only seem to stop by collapsing in an armchair in front of the television or endlessly complaining how stressed we feel. We put out so much effort to be successful that we get depleted.

Making an effort can expose the empty nature of self, of *I*, its phenomenal appearance and its emptiness, whether gross or subtle. The utter transparency of *I* stands revealed. We then breathe freely from one day to the next. Natural wisdom reveals natural freedom of the mind and an untroubled existence. No movement of the mind, one way or the other, will make any real difference to the stable nature of things.

We apply effort to accomplish certain ends, to achieve satisfaction. It is all very human. Effort and progress may be seen as going from a gross self to a subtle self. As our being becomes more subtle we respond effortlessly to develop and maintain the wholesome or overcome or avoid the unwholesome. As understanding deepens it seems much less like an effort. Our being effortlessly responds to the embrace of life and the realisations that it offers.

INQUIRY

1. *What is worth making a daily effort for and sustaining?*

2. *What are you cultivating for that purpose?*

3. *Are you moving towards enlightenment or the finite?*

4. *Is there a gap between what is here and now and fulfilment?*

Right Mindfulness

I was jogging along the narrow country lane near Gaia House. I stopped and leaned into the hedge to let a car pass by. Without looking, I stepped back on to the read, not realising that immediately behind that car was another vehicle. The driver of the second car had enough immediate presence of mind to slam on the brakes, missing me by inches. We can pay a heavy price for a momentary loss of mindfulness.

There is nothing that we can take for granted in this world, including the presence of our existence. We depend not only upon our acts of mindfulness but equally upon others' mindfulness for the continuity of our existence. To pay respect to life is to act in a mindful way, for we can then acknowledge the natural interconnection we share with each other. It can be an extraordinarily insightful practice to bring mindfulness to bear on the most ordinary activity.

We respond or react one way or the other to events. Mindfulness mirrors the inner condition of our life. Unlike our face, our heart can stay bright, clear and spotless. If we are to feel content with ourselves we must first look in the right direction, and if we look honestly within, it will influence our actions. But we also need to be clear about the world we live in.

We bring as much mindfulness and awareness as humanly possible to our body, speech and mind, commiting ourselves wholeheartedly to this. We realise that meditation is simply the application of mindfulness with a form. We sit, walk, stand and recline with a meditative awareness. Mindfulness of the ordinary alerts us to a lot more than usual and we experience the connection between one thing and another. We pick up signals, attend to the general and the detail, watch what the mind is doing. We remain vigilant whether we treat the activities of the mind as skilful or unskilful, wise or foolish. We then begin to feel very much in tune with the flow of life and experience the significance of the here and now. Grounded in the present, we are able to see the past and future with clarity instead of with clinging, fear or exaggerated expectations.

Some of the Buddhist traditions have fallen in love with mindfulness; it has become elevated to the hub of the teachings. Some teachers tell us that everything revolves around mindfulness. Buddhists practise mindfulness. They attend retreats on mindfulness, and share together periods of mindfulness. To be mindful is in danger of becoming the supreme practice of the teachings. When we make mindfulness central to the whole practice of the Buddha-Dharma we are in danger of watering down the teachings to a particular quality of mind – called mindfulness. The teachings point directly to awakening to freedom, opening the heart, and enlightening insights into the nature of things. Anything else means compromise; settling for less than the best.

We often treat mindfulness as carefulness. If we are mindful we are less likely to hurt ourselves, less likely to have an accident. This is an important feature of this faculty of the mind, but it goes further than that. Mindfulness practice enables insight into the personality structure to arise.

John decided to give care and attention to everything that he did that day from waking up to falling asleep. He treated all things equally. As he undressed himself for bed that night, he felt he had gone through one of the most important days of his life. It had been a full day, rich, diverse and illuminating. John had learnt a lot about himself. He understood that applying mindfulness reduced the idea of habitual routines. There was much to find out about himself.

PRACTICE

1. *Go to the kitchen.*

2. *Mindfully wash up, dry and then put everything away. Do it as though it was your last act on earth.*

3. *Notice any demands and expectations within during the process.*

4. *What's the response?*

There are moments of sudden awareness that transform our view of things. Who is washing up the dishes? Does the water also get credit for clean dishes?

Every feature of the Dharma is equally important. Exaggeration of one feature will be at the expense of others, as the teachings embrace a vast web of interconnection. To exaggerate one aspect of the teachings gives it selfhood, a special existence beyond its relative merit. The teachings remind us that any attachment to mindfulness, gross or subtle, forms views and opinions.

PRACTICE

1. *Walk slowly up and down for twenty minutes. What stood out mostly upon completion? Was it the act of walking mindfully itself or another issue?*

2. *If something keeps repeating itself in the mind, does it indicate a lack of insight?*

3. *Bring awareness to anything for a seven-day period. It could be spending time in nature; working with a state of mind; a daily exercise. What did you learn from the experience?*

There are times when we are extraordinarily mindful. A primary fuel for mindfulness is interest, an important quality which affects the relationship to activities. When we fuel this interest with desire, it can manifest in unsatisfactory ways. We can spend our whole lives wanting to get things finished. We get one thing finished only to move on to something else with the same approach, and end up only being mindful of what tasks we haven't finished. If we bring full awareness to bear on the process of living, then there are no beginnings and endings; only the indestructible nature of things.

Buddhist retreats emphasising mindfulness and depths of meditation are held throughout the world. For the outsider, it can look rather strange. People sit still, being mindful, doing nothing in particular. They walk very slowly, eat their food rather slowly, and observe noble silence. Some confuse mindfulness with being slow. It happens many times when people queue to wash and dry their dishes. Those waiting find themselves watching their minds as one meditator slowly, slowly moves the cloth over his or her plate. Mindfulness pays respect to the commonplace, but not at the expense of another's patience.

The challenge is to find the Middle Way that is liberating and respectful to ourselves and others. To be truly present in each moment transforms the moment. It doesn't matter where we are or what we are doing. The tendency to undermine or dismiss situations springs from a lack of mindfulness, an unwillingness to be really present to what the moment has to offer.

INQUIRY

1. *When are you mindful and when do you tend to be unmindful?*
2. *What is the significance of being here and now?*
3. *What does mindful sitting and walking reveal?*
4. *It is not possible to be mindful in every moment. When it fades what do you rely upon?*
5. *Is there a relationship between mindfulness and liberation?*

Right Samadhi

We do not have a work in the English language that translates the word *samadhi*. The most common translation is 'concentration' which fails to express the significance of *samadhi*. *Samadhi* refers to the mind that is steady, focused, present with calmness and mindfulness. *Samadhi* is a state of peace, equanimity and contentment. It is a significant contribution to living with wisdom.

To its credit, the Buddhist tradition rightly emphasises the importance of developing and training the mind. We engage in a series of exercises and practices using methods and techniques to cultivate and develop calmness. A key is meditation that mindfully employs the four postures of sitting, walking, standing, and reclining. These exercises contribute to emotional and psychological well-being, as well as subtle experience and the capacity to remain steady amidst the circumstances of life. This capacity then becomes available largely without effort.

We often notice the tendency to put off projects, initiatives and acts of creativity. We tell ourselves to wait for the right opportunity, convinced that we will be ready later. These perceptions may hold little or no truth. They may be an expression of the mind that lacks *samadhi*. Without *samadhi* we procrastinate or act indecisively or impulsively.

In such an unsettled mind there is little chance of remaining focused, steady and responsive. *Samadhi* enables us to turn our attention to an object, to go back to it again and again, without resistance or impatience. There are times when we turn our attention to an object simply because we cannot put off the task any longer. This is a further sign of lack of *samadhi* in our life.

With right *samadhi* we remain clear about the intention, attitude and purpose supporting the *samadhi*. As with the other guidelines of the Noble Eightfold Path, we can employ *samadhi* in unwise and unskilful ways. There are people who have a concentrated mind and are able to attend to an object of interest in a sustained way. But their motives may be questionable, and not in accordance with the spirit and the letter of the noble training and disciplines.

Samadhi contributes to seeing the object clearly even though there is nothing particularly exciting about it. Mindfulness of breath meditation is perhaps the most famous example of all; the breath comes and the breath goes. Steadfast presence with the breath allows all the brain cells to settle down so the mind sinks deeply and comfortably into the body. *Samadhi* acts as a remarkable resource for study, concentration on tasks and capacity to bring things to completion. It enables our heart to sustain service to others without getting burnt out and to keep present when dealing with the fires of life.

Susan had a tough job. She had to listen day in and day out to harrowing stories of violence and sexual abuse from women and children. At times she felt her emotions contracting and her stomach turning over. She could feel her resistance to hearing these stories and knew that she had to make *samadhi* her practice. I advised her to sit in the chair with bare attention to the contact of her backside with the seat. Back straight, body very still, shoulders relaxed with minimal eye movement. If standing in the courtroom, she should direct her attention to the contact of her feet with the ground. Immediately after a session with a client, or during silent periods, she needed to remember to breathe mindfully, particularly relaxing on the outgoing breath. Before calling another client into her office, she should wait two or three minutes to clear her mind through mindfulness of breathing. We cannot be respectful to the next person's problem if we carry memories, feelings and thoughts about the last person.

Some people are slow to begin a task but once it is under way can follow things through. Others have the initiative to start things but remain slow to bring them to completion, if at all. Others do things in bursts and go from being focused to becoming unfocused.

Without *samadhi*, the mind may fade and lose focus. In old age, the mind may begin to crumble and become increasingly more forgetful of the order of the flow of events.

Some people have a great deal of passion to do things particularly well so that they gain attention through such activity. But after a period they lose interest as the attention of others fades. All of this indicates lack of mind training, and reduces our opportunities to benefit ourselves and others.

We often attribute the responsibility for lack of *samadhi* to the task itself. 'Why do I have to do this?' the mind protests. We then produce a range of reasons why we don't start, go slowly, go quickly or never get things done. It requires practice with a capital P to develop *samadhi*.

Our society offers no training in these simple but profound practices. Education offers cleverness as a substitute. An old Thai master who had lived in the forest in southern Thailand for more than sixty years told me, 'The world will not destroy itself through ignorance but through cleverness.'

As we enter deeper into *samadhi*, we experience inner absorptions that ground happiness, joy, peace and equanimity into our being rather than these pleasant states being a momentary high. There is nothing esoteric about samadhi. We develop it as a skilful contribution to our inner life.

We observe four kinds of *samadhi*.

1. As we develop *samadhi* we become aware of what arises out of the mind. We then have the opportunity for much insight into the movement of *I* and *my*. We notice *I* or *my* arises in relation to objects, body, feelings, perceptions, thoughts and consciousness. When identified with one area, it is not with another at that time.

2. We experience *samadhi* as a stabilising force for emotional and mental life. There is no suppression here. It comes out of calmness, single-pointedness and the practice of equanimity.

3. We experience a natural *samadhi*, not in meditation but in daily life. This *samadhi* enables us to keep focused in the long term on that which matters.

4. There is a day-to-day *samadhi* that can be present throughout

the entire duration of our life. It is the outcome of awareness, self-knowledge and insight.

Morality gives support to right *samadhi*, which supports wisdom. Relaxation, a feature of *samadhi*, accompanies effort in the same way that sports people explore the fusion of relaxation and effort. In the discipline of the Dharma, wisdom is sovereign, not the pursuit of victory at any cost.

It is wonderful and precious to experience *samadhi*, to know a deeply contented and focused mind. To develop *samadhi* requires practice. Here are some suggestions:

PRACTICE

1. Go on a retreat which embraces the Threefold Training of morality, *samadhi* and wisdom.

2. Sit in a meditative posture once or twice a day, or at least three times a week, for a minimum of twenty minutes per session.

3. Turn the attention to an object that remains reasonable steady, like the breath, rather than pleasant music, for example, that makes the consciousness light.

4. Focus on the breath. If it helps, count up to ten in a relaxed way. If you lose attention, then return to number one.

5. Or say a mantra such as the word *'samadhi'* or *'here and now'*. To establish calm and concentration, stay still and focused. Make this a regular practice.

THE TRIPLE GEM

This sudden glimpse of invoked beatitude,
Like the lost chord of a sweet anthem,
This unhindered discovery that pervades,
Where expansion dominates passages of time,
And self is fleeced of misperceptions

Introduction

There are three jewels in life. The first is full awakening or Buddha. The second is the Dharma, that which points the way to awakening. The third is the *Sangha*, the gathering of people concerned with awakening.

The Triple Gem (or Three Jewels) serves as a focal point for many Buddhists. To take formal refuge in the Triple Gem is the initiation into Buddhism and to become formally a Buddhist. Those who wish to uphold and protect Buddhism place great importance on the Triple Gem. They say it is the entry into this religious tradition and a refuge against the ugly forces of the world. Buddhists – monks, nuns and lay people – will often chant the Triple Gem in the Pali language on a daily basis:

> I take refuge in the Buddha.
> I take refuge in the Dharma,
> I take refuge in the Sangha.
> For the second time
> I take refuge in the Buddha,
> I take refuge in the Dharma,
> I take refuge in the Sangha.

55

> For the third time
> I take refuge in the Buddha,
> I take refuge in the Dharma,
> I take refuge in the Sangha.

Traditionalists treat with disdain those who give Dharma teachings without any ceremony or ritual of initiation into the Triple Gem. They say that to neglect this emphasis on the Triple Gem is to secularise Buddhism and reduce the teachings to meditation practice. Others say that wholehearted dedication to awakening, to the Dharma as the vehicle and the *Sangha* requires neither ritual nor ceremony. It is the commitment to the Awakening, Dharma, and *Sangha* that truly matters, not identifying it with Buddhism. Non-Buddhists can benefit from the teachings as much as Buddhists. The Buddha was not a Buddhist, nor the founder of Buddhism. He taught the Triple Gem. He said it was more important to be clearly aware of impermanence than to take refuge.

The Buddha

The Buddha said:

> Rare is birth as a human being,
> Hard is the life of mortals,
> Hard is hearing of the Dharma,
> Rare is the appearance of Buddhas.

Buddhists are fond of engaging in recollections about the Buddha. They remember his selfless dedication to the enlightenment and liberation of others. From the age of thirty-five to the age of eighty he walked extensively throughout regions of North India, proclaiming the Dharma for all. He renounced the attributes of royalty and wealth and focused his attention instead on understanding the human experience and the utter resolution of the problems of life. His life and wisdom inspired generation after generation to let go of the mundane and to penetrate into the nature of awakening.

No wonder Buddhists world-wide love to chant the qualities

and virtues of the Buddha. Buddhists take refuge in the Buddha. In a formal chant they declare their devotion to him. It confirms them as Buddhists. Buddhist texts state that the Buddha is

> accomplished,
> fully enlightened, endowed with clear vision,
> with virtuous conduct, sublime,
> the knower of the worlds (heaven, hell and earth),
> an incomparable leader,
> and a teacher of gods and human beings.

The value of such recollection helps Buddhists to develop faith, trust, and confidence in the Buddha, his teachings, and the *Sangha*, that is men and women of noble wisdom.

Some Buddhist traditions have endeavoured to break away from this historical perception of a Buddha outside ourselves. These traditions point to the Buddha within. (*Buddha* literally means 'awakened one'.) Strictly speaking the Buddha lies neither within nor without. Awakening is being one with the nature of things. In this respect, the Buddha belongs neither to the past, nor the present, nor the future.

To take refuge in awakening, we do not have to believe in the existence of the historical Buddha or that the Buddha is within us. We may or may not have doubts as to whether we have the potential for awakening. It would be a pity if there was such an identification with these doubts that we allowed them to dominate the quest for full enlightenment.

Awakening to freedom and the vision that emerges from it shows the greatest respect for life. To take refuge in awakening means making it the first priority of life. It means dramatically reducing the significance in our life of the material world of gain and possession. It means that we remain determined that self-aggrandisement will hold no spell over our mind. It means that pleasure and privilege are less important in our life. Recognising the limitations of all of the above stands as a hallmark of wisdom.

The Buddha said:

> In the sky there are no marks,
> Outside (the Dharma) there is no Noble One,

There are no conditioned things that are eternal,
Enlightened ones are free from impediments.

The relationship to awakening varies considerably from person to person, tradition to tradition. There are some who believe that it is available and close at hand now. There are those who imagine that it is far away. Others will regard it as a long journey to be achieved after many lifetimes. When we consider awakening in terms of near or far, we engage in a measurement: essentially the *self* is measuring the *not-self*. The *I* then measures that which is *not of I*. It may have a pragmatic use along the path but needs our attention. Otherwise we can enter into the field of claims and disappointments.

The Buddha said:

> One who has gone for refuge to
> the Buddha, the Dharma and the Sangha
> sees with right understanding
> the Four Noble Truths.

In other words, we do not have to attach ourselves in any way to taking refuge in the Buddha in any religious sense. We do not need to perform a ritual for that. What counts is exploring the Four Noble Truths as a useful framework to understand existence.

It is important to remember that awakening expunges the mind of problems, and that the challenge of life comes out of circumstances, rather than from unresolved personal issues. Awakening illuminates one of the vial dualisms of life, namely *I* and *him* (or *her*), or *us* and *them*. We see from experience that where we cling we create separation and can make a world of enemies. It is true to say that awakening destroys our enemies. This means that we have dissolved the negativity and the hate that we transfer on to others or ourselves. Awakening makes us worthy and noble human beings. It is the mark of an authentically evolved person.

People have nothing to fear from awakening, yet some act as if they do. They fear it might turn their lives upside down. It might mean that their priorities change beyond the narrowly defined interests of self. It might pose a threat to any vested interest they have in their beliefs. All of this is true. But our resources and potential begin simultaneously to manifest to shake off the grip of any lingering fear and any clinging to a narrow view of our lives.

In awakening we realise the immense diversity of a universe that permits extraordinary tolerance. Awakening reveals a fusion of inner and outer tolerance. Sadly, the intolerant personality finds itself reinventing the wheel. The hub of this wheel is ignorance, and it generates inflated perceptions of self. The notion of self-importance gets propped up with various desires, longings and arrogant attitudes.

The Buddha said:

One who has passed beyond this quagmire,
this difficult path,
this wandering on from one thing to another
and delusion; who has crossed and gone beyond;
who is meditative, free from craving and doubts,
clinging to nothing; has attained Nirvana –
such a one I call Immeasurable.

We can go around and around the same issue for years, decades and even lifetimes, according to many Buddhists. The Buddha has not rejected nor disputed belief in rebirth. Just as birth acts as a seed for death, perhaps death acts as a seed for birth in the unfolding process of nature. The Buddha has frequently expressed concern about speculating about the past or future. He has not taken a fixed position that the force of life moves through different names and forms – like waves arising and falling in the ocean. At times, he has clearly adopted a provisional attitude towards rebirth. The Buddha said, 'The future has not been reached. Instead, with insight, see each presently arisen state. Let one know that and be sure of it, invincibly, unshakeably.' In this light, fixed views for and against rebirth have little relevance for the Buddha. Liberation ends the rebirth of the ego in the here and now. That's what matters. The teachings point to this realisation rather than views about past or future lives.

Awakening is neither the affirmation nor rejection of existence. Life is neither viewed as substantial nor insubstantial. To exaggerate the importance of our life or undermine it fails to see it as it is. To keep affirming life would be to overlook the ending of each moment, the ending of the day, the dissolution of our life. To reject or deny life overlooks the arising of the moment and the presence of life. Awakening neither takes up the view of clinging to existence, nor clinging to non-existence; neither to life nor to death. In this respect, awakening transcends such standpoints. There is no gap between transcendence and the here and now.

This reveals an incomparable freedom. One knows what needs to be known and abandons what needs to be abandoned. There is utter fulfilment. This is the Buddha mind.

INQUIRY

1. *Are you committed to awakening?*

2. *What do you need to develop in order to awaken?*

3. *What do you need to change in order to awaken?*

4. *What do you need to accept in order to awaken?*

5. *What risks are you prepared to take in your path towards awakening?*

The Dharma

We have a great love of knowledge. Some of it is useful for our existence, some of it is for entertainment, some knowledge simply fills up our mind with useless concepts. Out of fear of silence, stillness or non-doing, we may pursue ideas and concepts as a way to steer our mind away from facing itself or the bare facts of existence. We have become infatuated with conventional knowledge. There is also knowledge of the Dharma, but if not applied it is simply another theory about existence. True knowledge of the Dharma transforms our lives. It opens our heart, expands our awareness, makes clear purposeful action, and liberates the mind.

Dharma is one of the most frequently used words in the Buddhist teachings. It has a fourfold meaning:

1. The teachings directed to enlightenment.

2. Everything – material, mental, abstract or otherwise – is a Dharma.

3. Law, namely the law of dependent arising: the principle that

nothing can arise without suitable conditions for its arising, and correspondingly, nothing can pass without conditions being there for the thing to pass.

4. Duty; acknowledging and understanding the Dharma of one's life.

As with awakening, the Dharma teachings are worthy of our recollection and reflection, since we can experience and understand them here and now. They are timeless. They apply to all humanity no matter what culture or time in history. The teachings are also worthy of investigation and carry with them a sense of direction and purpose. They are inward-moving and can be known, experienced and understood by the wise.

The Dharma must be distinguished from conventional beliefs. We explore the teachings through the moment-to-moment movements of our daily life. We can know in this very life the full fruits of such an exploration. It has been noted for the past 2,500 years that the Dharma is beneficial in the beginning, middle and end. The teachings remain significant in their general approach to life and in their detail. These teachings reveal many different aspects of the Path to Enlightenment. The Dharma reminds us to attend to ethical foundations and investigate hindrances.

We inquire into the relevance of each factor of the Eightfold Path. The Dharma invites depth of meditation both for calmness and insight. It opens up consciousness, drawing out of us depths of *samadhi*, allowing joy and inner peace. The Dharma points to living with practical, down-to-earth wisdom in day-to-day life. It generates a degree of knowing and insight into the nature of things that is unshakeable. Yet the Dharma itself is not worth clinging to. It is a resource, a challenge and a tool for liberation. Just as a person climbing a high mountain takes one step after another, with each step leaving the previous step behind, until reaching the top, where all the previous steps are left behind. It is the same for Dharma.

We develop the capacity to explore the beautiful and ugly faces of daily life. It is a matter of opening up to the immense challenge of being alive. Dedication to teachings and down-to-earth practices makes liberation close at hand rather than a far-off discovery. With that in mind, the teachings act as an extraordinary challenge to any lingering selfishness, negativity and fear. In meeting this challenge, we can never fall back into the sleep of habitual existence and so these teachings provide dedicated people with all the necessary resources for unshakeable realisations. It is in this spirit that the teachings have been made available.

Over the years I have heard numerous accounts of people's experiences with certain gurus during *darshan* (eye-to-eye contact). But this is not a substitute for authentic *darshan* with daily life. *Darshan* means 'seeing'. *Seeing* into the characteristics of existence; *seeing* the liberating truth. Every person, great or small, belongs to the Dharma of the here and now. *Darshan* with the Dharma of the living present requires consciousness, but does not require the use of senses such as seeing and hearing. *Darshan* with the here and now remains available for the blind and the deaf as well as for those with good eyesight and hearing.

Being onward-leading, the Dharma does not rest on itself nor on its own merits or virtues. We may have to travel the earth to uncover the depth of these teachings. Or we may not need even to move from our chair to uncover them. We can start right here, right now, being mindful and conscious. We can come to love the Dharma. It is a sensible teaching for sensible people. We don't have to advertise it or knock on people's doors with leaflets.

There is no Dharma gospel, nor absolute authority, not even the Buddha. We may try to express the Dharma through language so that others may see if there are features of it that might be useful for them. The Dharma does not come as a package, but as a lifeboat to enlightenment. Experience counts. It also is not worth holding on to upon arriving safely on the far shore. When we give protection to the Dharma, the Dharma gives protection to us.

INQUIRY

1. *Are you willing to draw on the teachings that are specifically relevant to your situation?*

2. *What is the difference between beliefs and inquiry?*

3. *What do you regard as the most important teaching you have had in your life?*

4. *'Dependent arising' is an essential feature of Dharma teaching. How do you understand this term?*

The Sangha

The *Sangha*, which literally means 'gathering', is the community of like-minded people who share a love of the Dharma. Wisdom and compassion bring the *Sangha* together. The *Sangha* commits itself to intensive meditation, inner work, insights and full realisation. It cultivates letting go and deep friendship, and works to overcome suffering in the world. The *Sangha* is worthy of support, kindness, and gifts. It deserves hospitality as it is a force for the welfare, benefit and liberation of many.

It is also worthwhile to recollect the virtues and qualities of the *Sangha* to the same degree as the Buddha and the Dharma. In times of doubt or difficulty, people on the Path might reflect on the benefits of connection with the Buddha, Dharma and *Sangha*. Associations with wise and compassionate people help sustain the practice. To reflect on the *Sangha* of past, present and future can give further inspiration. We develop appreciation for this expansive network that contributes to living with love. The *Sangha* has no particular religion, no dogmatic standpoints, no flavour of being a cult or sect. It is found inside and outside religion. Wherever we find wisdom and compassion, we find the *Sangha*. The *Sangha* shares the view that greed, negativity and self-delusion need challenging.

This ability to reflect on the significance of the *Sangha* inspires love and happiness. We feel the strength of the *Sangha* and know it has continued for countless generations. We may experience, as it were, the descent of past Buddhas, Bodhisattvas, Noble Ones and saints, named and unnamed, into our being. We may hear their voices and feel their presence in our inner life.

For those of us who feel this connection, there is the heartfelt wish to contribute to the support of the *Sangha*, knowing such authentic support takes the pressure off the self. It is this association with the *Sangha* that enables us to step forth alone into areas of conflict. Even when the *Sangha* of one goes about his or her work to end suffering, the wise know that they are not really on their own. We will not get overwhelmed with suffering when linked to a tradition of wisdom. We know the foolishness of relying upon the conditioned self to respond skilfully to circumstances.

Some confuse the character of the *Sangha* with identification and clinging to a particular group, teacher, book or belief system. Traditional Buddhists will regard the religious order of monks as the *Sangha*. Others believe there is more than one tradition of the *Sangha*. The mind then becomes either divisive or confused. There is one tradition of wisdom and compassion, not two, just as in nature there is one formation called a tree, no matter how many different names we attribute to it. The *Sangha* consists of men and women of wisdom and compassion, of Noble Ones and those who practise to lead a noble life.

Buddhist monks and nuns dedicated to Dharma practice have a vitally important role in society. They remind us all of the importance of non-violence, contentment with little, meditation, emptiness of ego, daily disciplines, mindfulness and inner freedom. They provide monasteries that serve as refuges from the demands of the world. As servants of the Dharma, they also provide teachings for those interested.

Cults have a number of distinguishing features that bind members of the cult together. These features often include most or all of the following:

1. Attachment to a teacher, book or belief system.

2. Regular displays of intolerance or arrogance towards others.

3. Humiliation of those who ask questions that could make the leader or group feel insecure.

4. Feelings of superiority born from comparison with others.

5. An inability to support, endorse and appreciate the wisdom and compassion of others.

6. A wish to expand their spiritual empire.

7. Eviction of those who show doubt.

One of the cardinal sins of the Dharma life is to create a split in the *Sangha*. We train ourselves to be free from grasping on to the hostile and divisive views of self or others. Some people express the optimistic view that those who find their way into a cult will experience this for a particular phase of their life and then come out of it, but there is little evidence for this.

There is no shortage of those who honestly believe they alone have access to the truth and all others deceive themselves. The *Sangha* practises freedom from narrow mindedness. When grasping and identification take place, we become increasingly more intolerant. We hear Buddhists say people are poor and sick because of their karma. The implication is that they had done something bad in their past life to reap poverty and sickness in this life. Those who suffer deserve more understanding than such simplistic views. The *Sangha* practises seeing through the judgements that divide people.

The duty of the *Sangha* is to work diligently for the enlightenment of all, whether connected with the Dharma or not. There is much merit in making offerings to the *Sangha*, to people who love and care for the world. There are people who daily give their time and attention to the needs of a single person. Their selfless love and dedication reveal the mind of a Bodhisattva. Such Bodhisattvas go about their work anonymously. They belong to the *Sangha*. The *Sangha* of unsung heroes stands as the antidote to the selfishness and cleverness that haunts the earth.

The presence of the *Sangha* of wisdom and compassion upholds the earth, safeguarding it from becoming a hell realm. The *Sangha* of the Noble Ones matters to life on Earth more than we realise. The *Sangha* makes available the Dharma. Offered freely, the teachings are given on the principle that that which is freely given is freely received. Dharma teachers and senior practitioners receive the priceless Dharma freely from their teachers, so they give it freely.

Our priority is application of the Dharma to our daily life. If we always keep that in mind, we will not slide into factionalism. The *Sangha* does not own the truth, nor possess it. The *Sangha* cannot take up the truth, cannot organise it, and has no claims on it whatsoever. The truth does not belong to anybody. It does not exist in the hand of an individual or book. It cannot be measured. Humbled by such an understanding, the *Sangha* has nothing whatsoever to hang on to. Free from clinging, it lives in tune with the Dharma of awakening. The bare truth of this sets us all free.

Inquiry

1. Do you experience contact with people living with wisdom and compassion?

2. Do you feel isolated? If so, why?

3. Do you make space in your life for others?

4. Do you make the effort to attend meetings and gatherings of thoughtful people?

5. Are people all the same, different, both, or neither?

EIGHT WORLDLY
CONDITIONS

Dwell on your frustrations
In this space of past trials,
What you are doing with such intentions
Expresses an endearing futility,
Like the wind battering the sea.

Introduction

The liberating truth of things stands before us and we go on ignoring it. We find ourselves trapped repeatedly in the First and Second Noble Truths. What is also true is that it is a tragedy to waste our existence by identifying with any one or more of the following eight worldly conditions.

1. Profit and Loss.
2. Success and Failure.
3. Praise and Blame.
4. Pleasure and Pain.

It takes a considerable degree of honest inner examination to know if our life has become consumed by such obsessions. We throw away our existence in the vain hope of gaining profit, success, praise and pleasure while negating or minimising loss, failure, blame and pain. We might cling to the belief that on the whole we have had more of the first than the second. It might be true. It might also be true that we have had more of the second. Either way we can spend our life caught up in the Eight Worldly Conditions.

None of us can escape some contact with the Eight Worldly Conditions. These conditions belong to the periphery of what is significant. It is the ego, lurching into pursuing and grasping, that makes these Eight Worldly Conditions our ruling concerns. We can sleepwalk through life as though only profit, success, praise and pleasure mattered, but there is the opportunity to discover something of a totally different order altogether.

Inquiring into the Eight Worldly Conditions does not promote an other-worldliness. This inquiry allows the chance to open up our consciousness, to bring awareness to bear on existence. This will make a difference not only to our life but to life itself. Thus we need inner metal, true non-attachment to the gratification of the self, and passionate dedication to knowing the nature of non-duality.

Profit and Loss

Our cherished affluence is our undoing. We like to believe that having more luxury goods proves we are better off. We compare the past with the present. We look around and see we have more of everything, including labour-saving devices. But we have less free time than ever. We ought to be reflecting seriously on why this is the case, why we have no time for relaxation, meditation, play, clear-seeing or peace of mind.

We have no time to question what it means to be or to investigate the self. We have no time to enter into the poetry of existence. We have purchased so much, and yet have sold our existence.

Sam was a professional fund-raiser for a major political party. He travelled a lot, wrote a huge number of letters, and spent hours on the telephone. He concentrated on making as much money for the party as possible and worked extraordinarily hard. The more money he raised, the bigger his salary. Outwardly, his work seemed altruistic. After all, he worked for what he believed in. Inwardly, he knew differently. He had a large mortgage and an expensive lifestyle to maintain, and was obsessed with increasing his income.

Through conditioning, inner and outer, we get caught up in obsessive desires. We want more. More of everything. We lose appreciation of and satisfaction with what we have. Desires rule our life. Products have no power to fulfil desires or sustain them. All advertising should carry a mental health warning: 'Desire can damage your mental health'. Money, debts and security occupy too much of our attention. We fail to look at the arising of desire, the staying of it, the passing of it and the re-arising of it. When we dissolve the loop of desire, we discover clear and wise action.

We have come to live in a bizarre set of circumstances. We experience a void in our life through not having what we want, and thinking we haven't made enough profit, enough money. We fail to see that what society produces and promotes contributes to making this void in the first place. Goods cannot fill the void. The inner void becomes dependent upon certain goods; the production of many goods depends on the inner void. Unless we have gone deep, our life remains restricted to notions of having and not having, profit and loss.

If we fail to meditate on this, we'll go on living in heaven and hell. Heaven is getting what we want, and hell is failing to. It ought to be apparent to us that the contrived world of profit and loss is integral to desire and goods. Money is spent to create the goods. Money is spent to get the mind attracted to goods. We spend money to purchase the goods. Production creates desire. Desire creates production. All of this is elementary stuff but it still requires a depth of awareness and insight to stand free from entrapment. If we don't, we pursue an existence of constantly needing to make even more money. With greater disposable income, we can pursue more goods and security to try to fill a bottomless inner pit.

Crass displays of wealth and ostentatious living also become the means to impress others. It would appear that some rich people gain a strange sense of satisfaction through displaying extravagance in front of people who indulge in the same values. Deep down, we know there is something shallow about a grossly self-indulgent lifestyle. Occasional donations to foundations and charities make little difference to such questionable ways of living. Suffering, ageing and death make a mockery of living to excess. It is no wonder that the teachings point to the discipline of moderation, rejecting selfish consumption at the expense of the less fortunate.

We have elevated goods and information technology to new metaphysical levels. This keeps alive the pathology of profit and loss and the absurd belief system that increased production solves all social problems.

Many people believe:

If we increase production it will improve the quality of life.

If we increase production it will solve unemployment.

If we increase production it will lower crime levels.

If we increase production the poor will be better off.

If we increase production we will get ahead of other industrial nations.

If we increase production it will improve our standard of living.

Those who doubt this are treated as heretics of conventional wisdom, irresponsible and out of touch with the real world. We do not have to become austere ascetics. We do not have to become Buddhist monks and shave our heads. It is a matter of awareness and unconventional wisdom that sees the emptiness of this spell of producing and consuming. Our collective minds have created this god. The agent and the saviour to unite us with this god is money. Many people honestly believe that union with this god will save them from failure, loss and subsequent despair.

Richard lived on the West Coast of the United States. Every morning he got up very early to wheel and deal on the New York stock exchange. His stocks and shares were relatively safe, but fascinated with the world of profit and loss, he neglected his wife and children. He hardly gave them a goodbye as he made his phone calls from the telephone next to his bed. He tried to convince himself that he was gambling for his family, but they knew differently and resentment lingered in the air.

Mythology is the support structure for such a way of living. Our priorities need to change so we walk more lightly in the world. We make things last. We let go of concern with passing novelties, superficiality of competing fashions and the ego that indulges in endless pursuits.

We see societies that boast the greatest profit for certain individuals also show the greatest loss of benefits and support for others. We see that the two are inseparably bound together. State ownership has failed. Modest redistribution of wealth through taxation has failed. Relying on goodness and the philanthropic spirit have failed. We have failed to bring economic justice to the vicious cycle of profit and loss. The haves and have-nots remain locked in co-dependency. Our political masters, corporate leaders, economists and accountants remain trapped in the status quo. The problem is with all of us and within us all. So is the resolution. We have to work on it together.

INQUIRY

1. *Are you substituting the word ambition for greed?*
2. *Do you rationalise your addiction to profit?*
3. *What are the consequences for yourself and loved ones when there are sudden dips in profit?*
4. *If you get what you want what will it get you other than pleasurable sensations?*
5. *Do you own what you have or do your possessions own you?*

Success and Failure

I was standing outside a hall in the centre of a city waiting to give an evening talk. A man came up to me. He asked me if this was the place where Christopher Titmuss was speaking. I said, 'Yes.' He then said that two associates had recommended that he should come and listen to the talk. 'I'm trying to run a successful business. I'm working every hour God sends. I barely have time for my wife and kids. Have you listened to this guy before?' he asked me. I nodded. 'What am I going to get out of it?' he asked.

I said to him: 'Christopher can't do for you what you can't do for yourself. My advice is to go home, spend the evening with your wife and kids and stop working your butt off.' At that moment, I was invited into the hall. I went to sit on the solitary seat in front facing the audience. When the man saw me, he looked a little startled.

We become so attached to being successful that we fail to see the cost. Driven along by desire, we set ourselves endless goals. It is hard to break out of that spell, and it is a spell. Under the force

71

of conditioning, the mind gets firmly stuck in reaching objectives. Our motives may change – money, influence, security or good feelings. We may have forgotten why we do what we do. The reasons may no longer count. It may boil down to the fact that we can't see outside our conditioning.

If we have reached this point in our life, then the word *success* won't have much meaning either. Thoughts about changing our priorities carry no substance. By this time, notions of choice and free will seem absurd. Our life force is firmly fixed on its path even when others scream at us to change our ways. With no public debate about what success means, there is little likelihood of finding much space within for any inner debate.

By common consent we acknowledge that the degree of stress has increased for most people during the past generation. Things are not getting easier.

All the aerobics, mantras and therapies in the world won't fundamentally change things unless we take an honest overview of our whole way of living. Success loses its meaning when:

1. You lose a spouse or, often even worse, a child.
2. You go through a divorce or separation.
3. You fear major illness.
4. You lose your work or business.
5. You get into debt.
6. You face investigation.

Such experiences inflict stress that affects our sleep, diet, relationships, and thoughts of past, present and future. In the midst of all our troubles, we make strong resolves to change our ways. The crisis passes and we then fall back into our old ways and begin to get stressed out again.

We have to face stress. Stress is the collision of desire and fear. We want to get something done and we fear that we won't. We get trapped in these two inner forces and when both collide, we call it stress. For stress to stop, living in desire and fear must end. Stress invades every aspect of our being – emotions, thoughts, perceptions and even our cells. A genuinely successful life reveals a lack of stress, a depth of awareness, love, right action and liberation.

We would have to say that some of the most allegedly successful people are the least successful when it comes to living intelligently. Their world runs rampant with desire and fear, affecting
the lives of others near and far. This kind of life leaves people ill
equipped to deal with death, life-threatening sickness, divorce and
loss of success.

PRACTICE

1. *Learn not to rely on your initial reaction to a difficult situation.*

2. *Learn to place any problem into the wider scheme of things.*

3. *Search for the wisdom to handle situations well.*

4. *See the emptiness of the judgmental mind.*

5. *Keep questioning until you wake up.*

Success does not only apply to career, money and security.
Naturally, we want to be successful at whatever we undertake. If
our expectations for ourselves are high, we face disappointment,
and long-lasting regret. We can feel a failure through self-blame.

Mary, a nurse, told me she could never forget one particular
incident in the hospital. The doctors decided that the life of a new-
born baby weighing less than two pounds could not be saved. They
passed this tiny being, wrapped in a piece of cloth, to Mary for disposal. As she carried the baby, it began to cry, so she held it in her
arms. Suddenly a senior nurse came in the room and yelled at her.
The baby slipped out of her hands and fell to the floor. It stopped
breathing. Since that day, Mary had felt she was responsible for the
baby's death. The incident constantly troubled her. She felt she
was a failure.

Our mind leaps easily to conclusions about ourselves through
grasping on to results or effects of circumstances. I told Mary that
she had forgotten the purity of the intention to hold the tiny baby
until it had breathed its last breath. In such important matters of
life, intention is sovereign. But when our mind switches to results
and the end of the process, we can blame ourselves for the outcome.
When that happens, we get overcome with a terrible feeling of failure. Such feelings run deep into the emotions and we then become
constantly vulnerable to a lack of self-worth.

There is belief in success and failure through selfish intention and the ambitious ego. There is also belief in success and failure through wholesome intention and the caring self. It takes clarity to know the difference. Yet the emotional outcome can be similar through the self's dependency on results. One of the ways that we can see any attachment around success concerns thoughts of the future. Our mind can set itself up with a particular goal, with daily life focused on achieving that goal. No matter how well planned, there is no guarantee that the future lies in our hands.

If we were seriously to reflect that our success might mean other people's failure, it might alter our way of thinking. Those attached to success become convinced they live in the real world. Their reality is living in competition rather than living together on this earth. Competition, success and failure, for and against, are views born from divisive thoughts. It takes some insight to give up this view of existence so that our actions spring from our common humanity.

To let go of success and failure, to stay in touch with fundamental reality, shows wisdom. We keep our hearts open and learn to understand all those on either side of the divide of success and failure. The spell of success breaks. The fear of failure dissolves. Having touched this depth of interconnection, we act from that perception. There are more important things in life than the results of actions. Wisdom comes first and last.

INQUIRY

1. *What determines success?*
2. *Are success and self inextricably bound up together?*
3. *If you abandoned interest in success, what would be the quality of your life?*
4. *Does success in one area mean failure in another?*
5. *What is the success that can never be lost?*

Praise and Blame

Tara participated in a sixty-day retreat, which embraced silence with devotion to sitting and walking meditation. During the retreat, she observed within herself a pattern of needing the approval of others, a pattern that had troubled her all her life. She wanted others' praise and feared their judgement. She did not expect this pattern to arise so strongly in a silent retreat. The pattern showed itself in two areas. When she engaged in the slow, mindful walking meditation on the lawn, there were times when she would become conscious of others. She noticed she wanted to impress them. No matter how often she told herself that it did not matter what they thought or said, these thoughts still arose. I suggested to Tara that she was taking such thoughts too seriously. It is only natural to appreciate the recognition of others. Rather than trying to negate this particular tendency, I reminded her to carry it lightly. Very soon afterwards when she noticed the momentary reaching out for approval she began to smile within.

The second area the pattern showed itself was during her time in the kitchen chopping vegetables for the daily one-hour work period. She wanted to show the staff that she was a sincere retreatant by proving to them that she did her job well. She felt fear of not getting her task completed and thought that others would admonish her for her slowness. In this situation, she began developing the practice of calmness, letting go, staying true to her purpose, and not interpreting the mind of others.

It is not unusual for us to spend much of our life wanting to live in the world of praise rather than be subjected to blame. But we forget we are born with two ears. It would make good sense to reserve one ear for praise and one for blame and stay steady between the two The hungry mind has an alarming tendency to feed on both. Praise can act like a drug and blame like a virus.

We can find ourselves feeding on praise. We want to feel really good about ourselves so it becomes the underlying motive behind what we do. We clamour to get acknowledgement and recognition from others, feeling that we honestly deserve their affirmation. We talk constantly about how much we do for others and wonder why we are not getting the credit. It is all too easy to have a shopper's mentality around doing good for others: I give this to you (time, energy, money, support) and I want you to give me something in return. But what happens when our actions are not appreciated? Do we start throwing blame at others? If we do, we are admitting to ourselves and others our dependency on praise. Our little world of praise and blame will collapse around us, leaving us in a heap of disappointment and frustration.

The mind easily moves back and forth between the polarities of praise and blame. They become the reasons for our actions. We want approval and we fear disapproval. This stops us from seeing the merit of insight or the action itself. We are preoccupied with what people think about our actions, and therefore about us. In our uncertainty, we seek counsel from others. Some will tell us to take risks; others will tell us to be cautious. Their advice may help us to clarify a situation, to think of points we had overlooked, or their opinions may add to our confusion, but we like to think that we made the final choice. We often think it is the particular issue that matters. The issue itself has a relationship to the perceptions, feelings and thoughts we have about it. We may also have to look outside the condition of the perceiver and perceived. Issues around praise and blame reveal the outer edges of tendencies showing uncertainty, insecurity and the wavering self. All of this ought to be obvious but, more importantly, it helps us find solutions.

To remain clear between the forces of praise and blame means:

1. Being true to our insights and perceptions.
2. Developing the capacity to withstand criticism.
3. Associating with those for whom compassion comes before conformity.
4. Ensuring that our commitment is useful, steady and ongoing.

When we can't handle blame or the accusations of others,

a. We attack back,
b. Withdraw, *or*
c. Become defensive.

It is vital that we become aware which of these three tendencies predominates, and arrest that tendency. This may require strong resolutions.

(a) With the first tendency, attack, we want to reduce the size of the other person in our mind. We find fault, and dismiss what they say so that we elevate ourselves above them. This often means the exact opposite. In our reaction, we may have sunk to their level or even below them. The intensification of this is to kill someone, to reduce them to nothing. It may not happen in real life but it may come out in nightmares, ugly thoughts or fantasies.

(b) With the second tendency, when we are blamed, we feel hurt so we withdraw. We refuse to communicate, grow cold, detach ourselves, or resign from a role. The ultimate withdrawal is suicide.

(c) With the third tendency, we become defensive – going over our positions again and again. We feel misunderstood. As a result we go running from one person to another to gain sympathy, putting forward our position as much as possible. It rarely seems to work. We sound defensive. We are defensive. The murmurings of hurt, disappointment and guilt get communicated, while the facts of the matter become secondary.

Nobody living in this world can escape blame or the fact that what people say about us may contain a kernel of truth. If we have developed enough awareness and equanimity as part of our practice, we will be able to sort out the essence from the accompanying negativity. It might well be that blame, when heaped upon us, has an important insight or perception within it. It would be a pity to utterly dismiss the totality of the feedback. It would block the opportunity for some insight into ourselves.

Anybody who spends time in any role involving contact with others must be exposed to praise and blame. The greater the number of people we have access to, the greater the opportunity for others to express their views about us. Sometimes others' views are a pleasure to hear and thoroughly agreeable to our ears. We would have to be a dead fish not to appreciate such responses.

There are some people – such as parents, teachers, authority figures – who appear very reluctant to offer any appreciation to others, thinking it might feed the ego and be unhealthy. It is important to be able to distinguish between praise and appreciation. There is something distasteful in praising another to ingratiate ourselves with that particular person. To express appreciation enables us to focus on a specific matter, to acknowledge and communicate that precisely and accurately to the individual. There is nothing vague or over-the-top about it. Such appreciation generates its own joy and is certainly in accordance with the teachings.

Some people in the public eye get so much praise that they

claim to find it nauseating. They want to experience authentic communication rather than meaningless babble about themselves, yet they may be drugged on their own self instead of recognising adulation as worthless. Dependency on praise has an insidiously corrupting influence on our inner life, and it can generate self-doubt or inflated views of self-importance. It weakens our ability to deal with the non-pleasurable world that manifests in countless forms. Attachment to praise takes the joy out of being.

It leaves all sorts of impressions on the recipient and all sorts of painful outcomes at some future date. Seeing the emptiness of all this is a step towards liberation. Authentic joy comes with freedom from dependency on the views and opinions of others and freedom from self-doubt.

INQUIRY

1. *What is the difference between appreciation and flattery?*

2. *What is the difference between constructive criticism and blame?*

3. *Does the mind grasp praise and blame?*

4. *Does acclaim have a relationship to the self?*

5. *What is authentic joy?*

Pleasure and Pain

We can over-simplify our life. We often regard it as a movement backwards and forwards between pleasure, pain, and locations between the two, so it is hardly surprising when we get consumed with sensations, feelings and thoughts.

Pleasure appears as if it is the outcome of effort, a fruit of striving and determination. Yet we also know that what gives us a great deal of pleasure can also give us a great deal of pain. Some will conclude that it is a price worth paying, but in the midst of pain, doubts may arise about the price.

Smoking can be a metaphor for pleasure and pain as well as a real cause of it. We can smoke for three or four decades without too many noticeable side effects. There is pleasure in smoking six or sixty cigarettes per day, but at some point the body can take no more. Organs and cells begin to jam up through the overload of tar and nicotine. The cells will tolerate no more abuse, and begin to go awry. The fear of cancer and the suffering this produces can run for days, months and years. If the disease sets in there are probably very few who would say the years of pleasure were worth that pain and terror.

The woman had smoked two to three packets of cigarettes per day for thirty years. She turned up on the retreat with one intention – to kick the habit. Her voice had a rasp to it. Her heart worked overtime to draw oxygen into her lungs. Smoking had clogged her cells, prematurely aged her, and suppressed her emotional life. I suggested she drink pure, fresh water – morning, noon and night. Pints of it, every day, to wash her inner system. Every time the craving for a cigarette arose, she had to drink glasses of water instead. Months later, she wrote and told me she had stopped smoking.

The time gap between pleasure and pain can be long or short. Pleasure and pain are sensations. We experience pleasure as attractive, enticing and alluring. It pulls us towards things even against our better judgement. Thoughts may offer a token resistance yet we find ourselves pulled into what we want. When we have the power to witness the rise and fall of the desire, we shake off the grip of the constant search for different things to give us pleasure.

A Buddhist monk, a previous occupant of the cave in which I lived in Thailand, died in the cave. People from the village found his drawings beside him. One showed a smiling monkey swinging merrily from a branch. The caption read: 'Oh what happiness to know there is no happiness in the world.'

We have all known the experience of excitement about some future event. Our thoughts, projections and expectations get a grip on us. They are strong enough to stimulate cellular life, including goose pimples and flushes of excitement. There's a pleasure in all of that. Yet sometimes the arrival of the big day is an anticlimax. We wonder what we had made all that fuss about. The pleasure of the anticipation was greater than the event. The thought can have more potency than the event. If we pay attention to all this in our inner life we can learn a great deal about our sense of reality.

We often want to give meaning to our experiences. We imagine our perception is accurate and we look for causes to explain events.

Some will insist there is a meaning and purpose to everything. But such a strong view goes against our experience. We can experience such levels of pain, suffer so much abuse and injustice, that we can't see any meaning behind it. And why should we? If the hand of God is involved then let's cut it off. If we want to believe it is all part of the divine plan then there must be something warped about it. The graffiti on the back of the door of the public toilet said: 'God has given up on the world. He's now working on less ambitious projects.' There is much pain in this world with no purpose, meaning or reason behind it. It's simply pain arising because the conditions are there. Giving it reason or purpose may help us to resolve it or may not. Our conclusions may be accurate or bizarre.

One day a senior manager suffered a heart attack and was rushed to hospital from his home. Later, his wife telephoned the office to report what happened. The news visibly shocked the staff. One colleague said, 'The signs were there. He had been putting on weight and looked rather pale.' Another said, 'He certainly had been overworking. I know he stayed on after we left the office at night.' Another said, 'He never exercised. His wife told me he would just come home and slump in the chair.' Another said, 'I always felt that beneath his polite exterior there was a lot of pressure and unresolved problems.'

Two days later the same manager arrived back at work, bright and cheerful, much to the surprise of the rest of the staff. He hadn't had a heart attack after all, only a case of severe indigestion; he and others in a restaurant had reported the same intense discomfort to their doctors. Suddenly the staff had to revise all their reasons and explanations. They all felt extremely foolish and didn't know what to think.

There are some who genuinely tire of their engagement in the world of pleasure and pain. They perceive its limitations, sense it isn't leading anywhere, and know that it is a perpetual loop. Recognising that the years are passing by, there can emerge a determination to change their focus as they realise a world of pleasure and pain has no capacity to offer a fulfilled life. The greater the pursuit of pleasure, the more probable the invitation to pain. The more pain is faced, the greater the yearning to enter the field of pleasure.

In tiredness from pleasure or pain, we are vulnerable to reactivity. We can become impulsive, reactive and highly explosive.

Thoughts can arise that are out of touch with our current circumstances, sparking negativities, fear and depressed feelings. We give a reality to those thoughts; our views make us feel even more low. The pain becomes too much. All the pleasure has gone out of life.

Some travel through life in darkness about the way things are. It is like being in the forest at night and suddenly almost standing on a poisonous snake. Waves of fear, anxiety, rage and chronic indecision arise. Then we bring clear awareness to the situation. It's not a snake but the fallen branch of a tree. How could we make such an error of perception with all of its inner consequences?

Others may have a long, pleasant life. They do not have to face any snakes. This means that a pleasant state of mind has become their ultimate reality, but the final insult to this long, pleasant life is hoping to die in bed while asleep. The opportunity to inquire into existence was ignored. If we have to bend our existence to something truly worthwhile, then let us go towards noble realisations. Let us find out what it means to see things as they are.

Our practice teaches us to witness feelings as feelings, thoughts as thoughts, mind-states as mind-states. Insights into and understanding of pleasure and pain open out our consciousness beyond the limits of both. Realisation of liberation acknowledges the relativity of birth and death and the flow of events between the two. This is a timeless abiding that takes the breath away.

INQUIRY

1. *Do feelings constitute reality?*
2. *Do thoughts make reality?*
3. *Is reality a combination of those two or neither?*
4. *Do the experiences of pleasure and pain reveal reality or make it?*
5. *Do analysis and interpretations of experiments reveal the true nature of things?*
6. *What is reality?*

THE THREEFOLD
TRAINING

In seeing —
What utter joy!
The small mind becomes transparent, empty,
Without foundation.

Introduction

The spiritual supermarket is full of spiritual experiences, mind-body work, psychotherapy, the New Age, mysticism, Buddhism and countless books. In Dharma teachings the priorities boil down to the threefold training – morality, *samadhi* and wisdom.

There are some people who lead a double life. It is not that they have any malicious or egotistical intent, it is simply that they are attracted to being intensely involved with spirituality as well as with the Eight Worldly Conditions. They give a great deal of time and energy to both, wishing to have the best of both worlds. There is no shortage of gurus and preachers who offer both. Ultimately, though, one would be at the expense of the other.

This is not an unusual characteristic of the sincere seeker. He or she may attend retreats, workshops, and read the vast array of spiritual literature. A person may adopt a guru and engage in various spiritual exercises. There is a spiritual shopping list out there which can be fascinating, attractive, and mix easily and uneasily with the Eight Worldly Conditions.

The Threefold Training reminds us to keep our priorities clear so that we don't end up driving ourselves from one experience to another, one guru to another. Some go to India, California, the

Himalayas, Jerusalem and south Devon in the quest for enlightenment. All seeking deserves the support of the Threefold Training. The genuine Path to Enlightenment tempers the attraction towards spiritual narcissism. There is nothing superficial nor self flattering about waking up. It does not give an opportunity for personal back-slapping.

The Training serves as a catalyst to know the Immeasurable. We need to be vigilant that we do not become rigid about the teachings and practices. They are a serious commitment but not to be cultivated at the expense of joy, love and appreciation for the ordinary and everyday.

Morality

There is a difference between an ethical training and abiding by commandments. A major authority will impose commandments upon us. We either believe them or we don't, and there is a lack of opportunity to enquire into their relevance. Religious baggage also accompanies commandments. They cannot be separated from the book, the prophet or the saviour. Morality is of a different order. The outcome may be the same but the attitude is very different.

The Five Precepts, or ethical guidelines are a training in inner discipline. The training therefore is not a series of *thou shall nots*, but a code of practice:

1. I undertake the training not to kill.
2. I undertake the training not to steal.
3. I undertake the training not to cause sexual abuse.
4. I undertake the training not to tell lies.
5. I undertake the training not to abuse alcohol and drugs.

We can appreciate what a significantly different world it would be if people could only learn to practise respect for each of these guidelines without exception. It would be far more effective for us to pay attention to these Five Precepts than to indulge in our social/political/religious beliefs. The willingness to cultivate support for all Five Precepts introduces morality into our daily life.

This training in morality gives support and strength to the mind when faced with a challenge in any one of these areas.

It would be quite easy to claim that we *always* observe this code for wise living. We might say that we wouldn't dream of killing or stealing from one another. We might say that we would never hurt another sexually or tell a lie. But as a training, these guidelines go further than that. We would have to question our relationship to war, acts of terror by the state or the organisation, blood sports, animal experiments and the killing of insects. Stealing would force us to investigate exploitation, profiteering and taking advantage of others for our personal gain. We would have to examine whether or not we manipulate others for sexual satisfaction, or lie, gossip or backbite for conceited ends. We would need to look at our relationship to drugs and alcohol use and abuse, moderation and renunciation.

If we ignore these Five Precepts, we lose our way in life. We live out our selfish, egotistical tendencies regardless of their impact on others or ourselves. We live as prisoners to the vested interests of the self at the expense of morality. We can end up living a life in which we knowingly and deliberately seek to cheat, harm and exploit others. This lack of morality is a result of our unwillingness to confront our patterns of manipulation or denial.

We can look at the issue of money to understand how we must investigate further. Gaining sudden access to modest or substantial sums of money has its dangers. An inheritance, business deal, divorce settlement, compensation or money-making scheme can provide a sudden windfall. But then the mind might start looking at ways of making even more money. The ego skirts ethical considerations, with people near and far getting used or abused. Money, power and control feature strongly in the world of morality. Or the lack of it. Morality often comes under great pressure when money is involved. We can easily sacrifice so many thoughtful concerns when money gets into our hands. Desire and attachment can trigger detachment from any considerations of morality.

Secrecy also becomes a feature of an uncomfortable or questionable relationship to money. It is a sure sign that we have attributed to money a separate, unique and special existence. We talk about our money in general terms – but rarely reveal what we actually have. We are often more open about our sex lives. Money is still a taboo area. *Don't say, don't ask,* is the mantra.

We acknowledge that money has a value in relationship to other things, but we naively endow it with the ability to bring happiness, contentment and freedom. It is more likely that anxiety will ensue with fretting over money. Our perceptions become warped the more we establish the *thingness* of money. In fixing it as inherent and always desirable, money then corrupts our morality.

In some of the disciplined traditions of Buddhist monasticism there is a refusal to handle money. This discipline forces an austerity on such monks which is different from those monks who handle money for convenience. Wisdom comes before saying *no* or *yes* to money. Money itself is not the problem. It is our relationship to it. Are we using our money wisely? We can learn to give it a much lower place in our overall world-view rather than a central position. When there is inner contentment, we need to own and pursue much less.

Morality shows itself in dignity and protest. There are times when we marvel at the human spirit. Ordinary people can express a degree of morality that is breathtaking. The military had run a particular Buddhist country with an iron fist for decades. Informers lived in every village. In the city there were frequent military crackdowns on dissidents. Most people simply carried on with their work, sat in tea shops, or went shopping, but others felt outraged at their inhumane treatment at the hands of the military. They took to the streets, which meant summary arrest, beatings, tear gas, bullets, torture and imprisonment. The morality of such people often goes unnoticed. They are frightened and know the risks. They don't really think that their protest will make much difference. Yet they act. This is morality. These are the unsung heroes of the earth.

We can only develop if we cultivate a firm moral basis for our life. Meditation without morality is mental gymnastics. We need the encouragement, support and contact of those committed to ethical values. Morality is based on appreciating life. We don't wish to be killed, cheated, sexually abused, misled, or addicted to substance abuse. Nor do others. The basis of morality is simple – treat others in all circumstances as we wish to be treated.

We share much more in common than what separates us. We recognise the circumstances of others. Knowing that it's neither pleasing nor appreciated by others, we refrain from inflicting harm on them. We would not want it inflicted on ourselves. The training in morality is a constant meditation on these themes. When we live with such integrity it brings peace of mind. We sleep well at nights. We can look people in the eye. They trust us. We bring dignity and honesty to all our relationships. People turn to us in times of difficulty. With such morality, we can live with ourselves as well as with others. There is very little real awareness of ethical issues when we disregard others. Self first, others second, springs from misperception, misunderstanding. Morality springs from the awareness of interconnection, not from the domination of self.

INQUIRY

1. *What areas, if any, require immediate attention?*

2. *What are the resources for change?*

3. *Is there a willingness to end, once and for all, intentions to harm or exploit?*

4. *What pressures or views compromise your integrity?*

Samadhi

We might wake up one day wanting to do something meaningful for the world. We don't want to go on living in a circle of self and its narrow boundaries. It is not that we feel compelled to become a do-gooder. We simply want to express a noble calling. It can be unsettling to reflect on the flow of our life and our typical mindstream. In stepping away from the known, we are left facing the unknown, with the extraordinary opportunity to gain insights into its nature. All too easily, however, when we touch places of uncertainty we fall back on the old and familiar.

If we dare take risks, we can find immense appreciation for stepping into the unknown, going beyond the conditioned self. The true taste of the unknown can help us understand what freedom from the known and from form means. The transition from the known to the next known, from one form of life to another, can happen all too quickly. It would be creditable to explore the significance of the unknown next step before it becomes familiar in our life. We may never have that opportunity if we opt for safety and security above all else. Our relationship to the unknown matters, and our mental resistance to it prevents the opportunity for a vast array of insights.

The practice of *samadhi*, that depth of calm and concentrated attention, gives us the capacity to stay with the known and the unknown. Thinking of fresh initiatives can be very different from taking actual steps. Inspiration often tends to be short-lived. If so, we turn our attention to the mind and to the development of *samadhi*. If we look honestly at ourselves, we may find that we lack sustained focus. This means we are also not ready for sustained creative expression or dedicated service; neither do we have the capacity to express our vision. It may be that the presence of our egotistical self-doubting aspect hinders us. We have to be fired up to take steps away from conventional securities.

It might seem like a backward step to engage in the process of meditation before entering into the service of an interconnected life. *Samadhi* (concentrated attention) is a definite feature of people who keep calm and steady through circumstances. *Samadhi* acts as one of the finest gifts for meaningful outer action, giving support to vision, compassion, and a profound sense of interconnectedness. We need *samadhi* for that.

The practice of mind-training proves immensely beneficial for our personal, social and working life. It is important to remember that it exists with morality and wisdom. Without the other two the *samadhi* could become a form of concentrating *I* and *my*. Infected with *I* and *my*, the *samadhi* would generate successful selfishness at the expense of wisdom. It is not surprising that one of the strongest attractions to Buddhist practices is meditation. It is often the first stepping stone to deep inquiry into realising wisdom and removing this selfishness.

When you become exposed to different meditation practices and exercises, you begin to see the enormous range of meditations available. Different meditations serve different purposes. Worthwhile spiritual traditions offer meditation to transform consciousness, open the heart and bring clarity to perceptions. Buddhist meditations systematically offer detailed methods and techniques to enter into the depths of the mind.

For dedicated long-term meditators, the depths of *samadhi* allow altered states of consciousness. Perceptions as well as states of mind become increasingly subtle. In the deep sense of well-being, free from fear, consciousness supported by *samadhi* can experience different realms. There is an opening of the divine eye of consciousness. These experiences include out-of-body experiences, astral travelling, contact with heavens and hells, and knowing the presence of bodiless beings. Certain rare expressions of *samadhi* allow multiple *I's* to enter consciousness, or allow you to hear voices in walls or in nature, see angels and devils, see new colours, hear new sounds. *Samadhi* allows memories unassociated with this present existence to travel through consciousness, releases impressions stuck in genetic make-up, and shows probable future outflows from the streams of the mind. A crude analogy would be tuning into completely different radio stations. This is all rather normal and natural in the light of certain kinds of *samadhi*.

Samadhi, together with inner well-being, treats these experiences as natural and healthy. They attest to the power of consciousness to pass through conventional material perceptions of existence. There is much to learn and see from these experiences. They are useful resources for working with, and knowing, the expanse of the human mind. Some confuse these kinds of *samadhi* with mental disorder. Others confuse mental disorder with *samadhi*. In most cases, the difference between the two is obvious. For some it means more meditation to explore further. For others it means medication to eliminate the experiences altogether.

Meditation training gives support to a natural *samadhi* in daily life.

PRACTICE

1. *Be aware of stillness before movement (e.g. let the telephone ring three times before moving to answer it).*

2. *After a meeting, experience silence.*

3. *In the midst of doing, pause, and mindfully breathe in and out.*

4. *Practise feeling the aliveness of your whole being.*

Meditation can work through focusing on a particular object, known and familiar, arising out of the immediate field of existence. We attend moment to moment to an object in order to establish the combination of mindfulness and concentration. It could be the breath, sounds, a candle flame. With such focus, we leave out interest in all other phenomena. We find a depth of calmness, a sustainable presence and steady observation. Focusing inwardly can contribute to our capacity to be concentrated in matters of daily commitments and vision. We must be watchful of feeding issues of control – using will-power to stay attentive and forming lines of tension in the mind through trying to keep out thoughts. At times we can feel the body and mind pushing too hard. We learn to relax slowly into the process so that energy and presence flow freely together.

We can also expand our awareness to a meditation that embraces all objects. This choiceless awareness cultivates a sense of unity, spaciousness and natural intimacy with all things. The experience contributes to appreciating the importance of openness, relaxes the whole being and shows that nothing is worth holding on to. In choiceless awareness, we perceive all things in an equal light. We notice what the *I* alights upon – whether sights, sounds, contact with body, memories, plans or states of mind. We experience this choiceless awareness without grasping or clinging on to anything.

We must be watchful of building up tension in a focused meditation. We must be watchful of not getting spaced-out in choiceless-awareness meditation. In both meditations, the object or objects of interest reveal awareness, and awareness equally reveals objects. Both stand mutually supportive. In this relationship, where life co-exists, there is much opportunity for non-dual realisations and liberation. In calm, clear abiding no self arises; no personal storyline, no roles, no inner issues nor beliefs. The world of self becomes irrelevant. The focused or expansive experience of not-self releases contentment, sublime joy and effortless presence. *I* and *my* may arise for simple communication purposes, not problematically.

Samadhi makes our mind like a mountain in a hurricane. *Samadhi* enables us to stay steady, in touch with the processes of birth, ageing, pain, dying and death, whether in ourselves or others. We imagine that if we keep meditating, keep concentrating, we will reach the ground of being, but there is no finality to the depths of meditation. The insights emerge from seeing clearly. They can occur through the everyday ordinary mind or in the depth of meditation. The potential for immediate realisation of the non-dual always stands available. Insight and understanding confirm liberation. It can occur as a sudden breakthrough or in a gradual way. The light of realisation takes the substance out of *I* and *my*.

INQUIRY

1. *What time are you willing to devote to developing* samadhi?

2. *What do you most concentrate on daily?*

3. *What gives you joy as a result of focused attention?*

4. *Have you experienced a depth of* samadhi *that is truly illuminating?*

Wisdom

We have become servants of the grasping self which inhibits a wise life. Wisdom belongs to awareness, skill, generosity of spirit and liberation. We often narrow our focus in life to three areas:

1. Self-interest. This becomes the bottom line for every consideration and every action. 'What's in it for me?' governs our behaviour. We put ourselves first instead of understanding the interconnection of things.

2. Exclusive interest in the family. We marginalise many more distant relatives, friends, worthwhile causes and the poor. Making money for my family becomes a comforting thought. We believe that a large salary will benefit the family.

3. The interests of the nation. Living in a world of *us* and *them*, we identify intensely with our country. Taking this to an extreme, we become xenophobic, or we support declarations of war. We are always on the right side to justify killing men, women and children from other countries.

From the top level of government to ordinary citizens, there is a common determination to bring about wealth as our primary duty. Even children, when asked what they would most like to be often reply, 'I want to be a millionaire'. The priority of life then becomes a *taking* mode. We have become locked into this intense value system. We wonder where the wisdom is in this priority.

Many people read newspapers. There is a certain satisfaction in being well informed about the state of things at home and overseas. News mostly consists of reports of various forms of suffering manifesting around the world, with some analysis of causes and conditions. The news consists of exposing the first Noble Truth ('There is suffering'), but makes little reference to the other three. Wisdom concerns itself with all Four Noble Truths equally

It is unlikely that all newspapers, television and radio stations will *deeply* inform us about suffering and its resolution. We are told about suffering in the lives of people, animals and the environment but this does not seem to draw out of us compassion and determination to change. We might describe ourselves as living the illusion of knowing but not knowing. To know is to act. If we really knew about the state of the world, we would respond to it. It is the same with our unresolved inner problems. There would be no choice about it: we would be a force for change.

Wisdom supports morality and meditation, and vice versa. When we reflect on circumstances, we can develop four features of the Dharma for our collective well-being:

1. Awareness brings clarity.

2. Insights emerge from inquiry.

3. Meditation steadies the mind.

4. Action springs from vision.

If we attend to each of these four it will safeguard us from much confusion and conflict. Our capacity to stay steady enables us to keep action, insight and vision alive. We thus pay respect to ourselves and to life itself. This wisdom shows that we are on the right track. At times we deserve criticism for what we do or what we do not do. We need to hear the words so that we can respond to their essence.

Meditation is a key to change. We can meditate on the perception that, 'This is not mine, this I am not, this is not myself'. Reducing selfishness opens space within to see the world more clearly. Initially the thought might arise that such meditations lead to disillusionment with existence, yet things tend to work the other way round. Those afraid and disillusioned with existence tend to cling to it. Whatever we grasp on to we will have to let go of. The practices of non-clinging and association with those who know the wisdom of interconnection enable us to release love into the world.

In this non-clinging wisdom there is freedom from dependency, freedom from wavering back and forth. A genuine, effortless calmness runs to the very depth of our existence. Acknowledging this, we realise freedom from prejudices, born from clinging. We realise the end of bias, the end of the gulf between *me* and *other*. We know what is in common between us. Wisdom springs from this realisation. We know humanity before political, religious and cultural labels. Then there is no basis for inflicting suffering.

We realise the immeasurable nature of the heart and what it means to see things as they are. Through insight we see that which is clung to is conditioned and unsatisfactory. We tire of living caught up in this way. We stop sowing seeds of unrest in the present which lead to more unrest in the future. We sustain the first priority of finding liberation, which leads to the cessation of unsatisfactory formations. We experience gratitude for seeing in an undistorted, untainted way.

As we practise, we are not afraid to ask ourselves: 'Where is the wisdom to deal with this situation? What is a wise response?' We listen attentively for any message arising from the depths within. Rather than just foolishly going along with the conditioned mind, we listen to the voice of wisdom and sanity within. At first, it may not be clear. The wise voice may not emerge out of the murky depths inside us. Our only response may be: 'I don't know.' When this occurs we may have to keep faith with that voice rather than go along with the old reactivity that makes problems in life.

It if still seems a struggle to resolve a problematic situation, then we can try to find the wisdom elsewhere. We need to be careful not to be drawn to a merely sympathetic voice, but be prepared to hear the truth. There is wisdom in this world. It can be uncovered. Let us not sleepwalk through this existence.

PRACTICE

1. *Know contact with the world through sight, sound, smell, taste and touch. Experience the senses without the desire to fix or substantiate anything.*

2. *Abide with choiceless awareness through experiencing a deep sense of intimacy with all things.*

3. *Allow your whole being to rest in this choiceless awareness.*

4. *Neither indulge in memories, nor pursue future dreams, nor look for something to happen in the present.*

5. *Do not cling to standpoints that interfere with supporting an expansive vision.*

6. *Allow claims and possessiveness over existence to fade away.*

7. *Permit a transforming silence and stillness to pervade your being.*

8. *Embrace past, present and future, known in Dharma as the three fields of time.*

9. *Realise the emptiness of claims on things and experiences.*

10. *In this receptivity, regard any liberating insights into truth as expressions of truth rather than fruits of self effort.*

FIVE AGGREGATES
OF A HUMAN BEING

Who am I now?
Before my mind moves to respond,
Before the defining thought,
Before the stated view
Of warped assurance of self-existence.
What is this precious unbecoming
That my mind hurries to obscure?

Introduction

Who am I? What am I? Am I? To explore these questions, we don't have to thing up an esoteric reply. We can simply attend to ourselves in the areas which matter. The Five Aggregates of Human Being cover every feature of our life as we know it directly. We can speculate about a soul or divine essence. But such forms of language can be a distraction to the immediate and familiar sense of who we are. In Dharma teachings, *I* and *my* can be identified with the Five Aggregates:

1. Material form.
2. Feelings.
3. Perceptions.
4. Mental formations, thoughts.
5. Consciousness.

This is the basic composite of a person. The notion of *I* or *my* arises in relationship to all five aggregates, with nothing outside them for *I* or *my* to take up. Teachings and practices encourage us to be aware of where the *I* or *my* settles. We witness what happens to the

94

condition of the Aggregates under their influence.

All these Aggregates or composites are interdependent. We direct awareness to each of these Aggregates since they serve as a key to knowing about ourselves. We interpret our personality and our personal storyline through the various expressions of the rising and passing of combinations of the Five Aggregates.

We learn to track the arising and passing of the Aggregates in conjunction with each other. We do not treat them as separate self-existent entities but as interdependent. One Aggregate needs the support of the others.

We might say that such inquiry takes the *I* out of *I*, the *my* out of *my*. Insight dissolves the ego that generates problems in our lives. The Five Aggregates then rest in freedom rather than in ignorance.

Material Form

The first of the Five Aggregates is called *rupa* in Pali language, which means 'material form'. In the Five Aggregates, *rupa* refers primarily to the body. The form of our body influences the rest of us. The remaining four Aggregates influence the body.

Western science continues its fascination with the analysis of human beings. Neuroscientists and psychologists turn their expertise towards the relationship of the brain with the body. Scientists explain emotions and mental states as the 'firing of large sets of neurons'. Experiments in molecular science reveal links between the immune system and the brain. The immune system and the brain send messages to and from each other, in-fluencing our health. Science explains how our life functions between mind, brain, and body. To be a truly conscious human being, however, means more than theory, analysis and laboratory experiments. It means conscious application through personal experience. We can explore the relationship of body and mind through meditation.

Scientists realise that the lines of communication between brain and body get affected by abuse of alcohol, drugs, smoking and any form of substance abuse. Worry, loneliness and despair have an impact on organic life, affecting sleep, diet, exercise and attention to the body. When we get embarrassed our face goes red. We can get ill through ignoring or losing connection with the signals indicating forthcoming sickness. We can conclude that the cure for illness comes exclusively through medication, because we only look at the physical element. Meditation contributes to making the interactive flow of communication between brain and body as clear as possible. In a sudden life-threatening situation, our attention and awareness increases dramatically. We become acutely aware of the living organism of the body. We may even wake up to areas of our life that we have neglected.

Scientists tell us that the brain secretes a hormone at the time of danger that stimulates not only the body, but consciousness as well. It acts as a potent resource to bring awareness to the forefront. It is a pity if we have to wait for a life-threatening or intensely demanding situation to contribute to our waking up. Surely being born, ageing, feeling pain and dying ought to be enough.

Accompanied by a healthy mind, our immune system contributes to the elimination of foreign pathogens from the body. A clear consciousness and steady mind could also help tackle unsatisfactory cells, pain and discomfort. Then the body, brain, mind, consciousness, central nervous system and immune system would co-operate. There would be a vigilance around what arouses insecurity, fear and anger. We would learn from their impact on the body, and there would be an understanding of the way body sensations expose states of mind. All of us, including the scientific community, need to practise meditation so we can develop love and calmness, and know first-hand the physiological benefits.

For the most part, scientists seem reluctant to enter into such practices, to apply exploration of consciousness in daily life. Such things do not quite fit into their convenient language of analysis. If consciousness was brought fully into Western science, it would mean personal transformation for every scientist, every professional. The bringing of consciousness to bear on the body and states of mind through meditation enables us to develop our capacity for wisdom, for intelligent living. I believe advances in scientific and philosophical theory are no substitute for practical awareness and clarity about our condition.

It is useful to consider the body's outer appearance and inner actuality. We have become preoccupied, if not obsessed, with outer appearance – age, weight, size, measurements. We live in a narcis-sistic world where the mirror provides the opportunity for judging and comparing. All of this is involvement in the outer. The desire to feel satisfied about ourselves and impress others imprisons us in outer appearance.

We have spent far too much time looking at ourselves in the mirror, using the reflection to form all sorts of judgemental views about ourselves, both positive and negative. We invest much atten-tion in the condition of our face and the other parts of the body. It is as though our body along will determine the way people feel about us. Large or small, the mirror becomes a bizarre method to assess ourselves.

It is not unusual for half the population to carry a little mirror on a journey. It may be a blessing to smash this mirror into multi-ple pieces – let the broken glass reveal impermanence of all things instead! We spend too much time looking in the mirror.

We take care of the body's basic necessities including food, clothing, medicine and protection from the weather. When we cut through the preoccupation with the outer body, we contact the inner body that consists of physical elements, of vibrations, sensa-tions, the very life-force of the body. The greater the capacity we have to experience directly the elemental body, the less we will obsess about appearance. We then have the opportunity to strike a balance between care for the inner and outer. If we cling to the outer we will despair. No amount of hair transplants and cosmetics can cover up what is obvious to others and ourselves.

Direct access to the brain and the networks of the body is pos-sible through single-pointed focused meditation on the body. We can find out a great deal from first-hand experience. Direct medi-tative attention to the body opens pathways to understanding. The body of form, movement, energy, vibrations and sensations offers insights into mind-body relationship and the influence of con-sciousness upon the process.

MEDITATION ON THE BODY

1. *Direct the attention to full awareness of the direct body experience. Awareness of subtle and gross body sensations cuts through much of the projection, and obsessions, around bodily appearance.*

2. *Moment to moment, slowly scan from the head through to the toes and from the toes to the top of the head. Experience directly the sensations and vibrations of the body.*

3. *Notice areas in the body where there is tension, pressure, aches and pains. In a relaxed way, direct mindfulness into these areas. Be aware of the centre of the discomfort and also the outer edges. Observe the changes and impermanence of these sensations. Direct mindfulness also to areas where there appears to be a lack of sensation.*

4. *Return attention to full awareness of the whole body. Experience the body as organic life, as various vibrations and sensations touching on consciousness.*

5. *Ground yourself in direct bodily experience. Be mindful of descriptions and interpretations of the body through likes and dislikes, health and sickness, so that you can respond with wisdom to bodily life.*

6. *Experience mindfulness of body as the interdependence of the five elements – earth, air, fire, water, space – i.e., firmness, lightness, warmth or coolness, fluidity, spaciousness.*

7. *Realise the body belongs to the nature of things rather than being 'I' or 'mine'.*

Feelings

It is too easy to get into a situation where we put all the responsibility for our vulnerabilities upon our childhood. We will say to ourselves and our therapists, 'I didn't receive enough praise in my childhood' or, 'I was always scolded and blamed in my childhood. This is the reason I am the way I am now'. Who is making the judgement? We can use childhood as an explanation for our current state of mind. We may be accurate, but seeing the consequences of childhood conditioning may do much or little to transform our daily anguish.

While our bare feeling arise as simply pleasant, unpleasant or in-between, our emotions are more complex. Feelings become emotions when they become intensified through perceptions, imagination and memory. A single event often excites our emotions. We often experience our emotions as a force that can be healthy or unhealthy: fear, anger and grief become painful emotions, while love, joy and compassion become signs of emotional health. When a situation touches us, we often experience the wish to act, to respond. This may show wisdom or dangerous reactivity. A healthy mind stays in touch with the range of feelings and knows the healthy arising of emotions in particular situations.

It is important to learn to talk about our emotions, past and present. It is equally important to be committed to transforming unsatisfactory emotions. We sell ourselves short if we just talk about our feelings on the one hand, or never talk about them on the other hand. If we uphold a family tradition of keeping feelings to ourselves, two beliefs contribute to this emotional posture. We believe it is important to remain in control of our emotions. We worry what people will think if we bare our soul. It is our self-image at stake. Some hold on to the idea that showing emotions reveals a weakness. If anything, it ought to be the other way around. Refusal to show emotions shows lack of courage.

The second belief that contributes to holding back takes the position that nothing is wrong. Business as usual. But this is denial. It may be a tragic situation that is hard to face. The only way around it seems to be to act as if nothing has happened. The emotions are pushed back into our psyche. This makes for a very stiff personality. We may be able to stave off the emotion of sorrow, for example, but the suppression of such emotions with also stave off joy and happiness. There will be a solemnity about life, an inability to communicate with loved ones, and not much real enjoyment concerning anything. Those who cling to either belief may claim that emotions are a private matter. They could not be more out of touch. Such deep feelings need expression. They show a sense of connection with others.

Stephen had participated in numerous workshops, worked with a therapist, and attended retreats on loving kindness. He realised that there was a gap between him and his parents. In his mid-twenties, he felt he had never really connected with his parents. There were things from the past that still hurt and things he remembered with affection. He decided he needed to talk to them. Both parents clammed up. 'Past is past,' they said. He beseeched them. They ignored him. He said he felt they were still treating him like a child. They were still telling him what to do with his life.

Stephen's parents could not hear the voice of their son because they were unable to listen to their own feelings. Thus it was virtually impossible for them to listen to Stephen, no matter how important the issue was to him. Afraid of showing our emotions, afraid of the response from others, we cling to neutrality. There can be a dismissal of anything that shows intimacy and vulnerability. Perhaps deep down we are afraid to open Pandora's box, so we sit firmly on it. This attitude is far more damaging than sharing our feelings, our emotions and experiences.

One deep and open communication can be remarkably healing. Family members, partners or associates can understand each other, and it is a pity to deny the opportunity for such communication simply through clinging on to the view that everything is all right and there's nothing to talk about.

Stephen tired of listening to his parents' lectures about his lifestyle. He went home less and less frequently. His parents could not understand why. It hurt them but they would never admit it. They simply blamed him for not telephoning or visiting.

Sometimes our emotions are close to the surface. We might experience trepidation in picking up the phone, opening a letter, meeting somebody who is judging us. I remember years ago being savaged at a political meeting when I was standing as a Green Party candidate for Parliament. Four or five people subjected me to a fair degree of verbal abuse. Naturally enough, I didn't agree with them nor with their conclusions. If we trust our values, then we can hear words passing through the air, even if directed with hostility at ourselves. There are only words. It does not have to be that upsetting.

There are some people who wish to be controversial. They like to claim that they are free, that they can speak their mind, that they are not afraid of controversy. This is another way for the ego to seek self-satisfaction. Such people want to be talked about. They crave recognition and believe the only way to secure it is by appearing to be controversial. Their emotional life gets satisfaction through securing the attention of others. They prefer to be disliked rather than ignored.

This behaviour shows we are dangling on the edge of other people's views. There is still a wish to be noticed, to be affirmed by others. The mind desiring the attention of others is on a downhill slope ending in muddy waters. The controversial becomes the familiar and the forgettable. Living with wisdom, we pursue neither controversy nor conformity. There is an inner freedom when we express clearly and skilfully what we feel.

PRACTICE

1. *Acknowledge feelings whether pleasant, unpleasant or in-between. Feelings give support to activities of body, speech and mind.*

2. *Experience what is felt here and now. Is it pleasant, unpleasant or in-between? Stay quietly in touch with this feeling.*

3. *If the feeling intensifies and becomes emotion — ecstasy, sorrow, excitement, fear, bliss — let the experience unfold without struggle.*

4. *Neither detach from feelings nor encourage them. Do not fight difficult emotions, flee from them, or indulge them.*

5. *Acknowledge feelings of love, friendship, compassion, gratitude and equanimity. Be conscious of and receptive to their presence and expression.*

6. *Be mindful of interpreting past, present and future in the face of pleasant, painful or in-between feelings.*

7. *Be mindful of the interdependence of feelings and thoughts.*

8. *Clinging to pleasant feelings leads to desire and the pursuit of self-interest. Clinging to unpleasant feelings leads to withdrawal, aggression or other forms of reactivity. Clinging to in-between feelings leads to ignorance, apathy and blindness to the way things are.*

9. *Recognise the difference between spiritual feelings that contribute to ethics and wisdom, and worldly feelings where ego interests are paramount.*

10. *Realise that liberation is where perceptions and feelings have no foothold.*

Perceptions

A little boy picked out a large red juicy apple from the fruit bowl. He touched it, smelt it and tasted it. Through each of the senses, he recognised it as an apple based on his past experience. We call this recognition a perception. Feelings, thoughts, memories and habits influence our perceptions. When we develop clarity of mind through the practice of meditation, we perceive the way our mind moves. Seeing this reduces our conditioned reactivity to things. We see that getting caught up in attitudes for and against shows a dis-ease of the mind.

The outer life has its impact upon the inner life. The inner life has its impact on outer world events. There is a meeting of these two. This is contact. We experience the arising and passing of contact. Perception, feelings and the range of human experience arise out of contact. We frequently notice how easily our perception of a situation or a person or ourselves gets distorted. This distortion in perception affects our feelings, thoughts and attitudes. It also distorts memory. We say we can't change the past, yet the past appears to change when our perceptions change.

Due to the distortions:

1. We experience seeing permanence or continuity in impermanence. We believe something will continue and it doesn't. There are no guarantees of continuity in this world. Promises, contracts and vows cannot ensure continuity.

2. We experience satisfaction in the unsatisfactory, but habits and addictions compel us towards what our minds may know is unsatisfactory. We become helpless in the face of this distorted perception.

3. We experience self in the non-self. We think each of the Five Aggregates is 'who I am'. Causes and conditions give rise to mind-body, not the appearance of *I*. The *I* is not one with the Five Aggregates nor separate from them.

4. We often find ourselves having to revise our previous perceptions of a situation.

It is the inflation of particulars or the general that distorts perception. The distorted idea of what is good can be applied to any situation. We experience distortion of perception when we experience good in the not-good. We can apply our distorted perception of what is good to anything. In Dharma language, the good primarily relates to the Threefold Training and the Four Divine Abidings. When we forget this, we can justify any action as good on the grounds of our personal beliefs.

Karl thought it would be good to get to know a woman in his office. He could perceive her attractive figure and he liked what she had to say. He felt the trigger of particular feelings. He knew she was committed to another. He also knew that she had some measure of curiosity about him. Wisely, he made an agreement with himself that he would not take one step towards her. This perception of the situation became a source of protection for both of them. Clear perceptions enable us to see what is beneficial and skilful and what is not.

Karl said his spiritual practice in the office was observing the rise and fall of his desire for her. He knew that wanting her showed a distortion of perception. We get caught up in perceptions of *mine* and *not mine*. Willingly or unwillingly. We cannot perceive clearly when we get caught up in the arising of desire. Wisdom takes substance out of the *I* and *my*.

Perception also matters with spiritual experiences. John had worked in an office for most of his life without ever thinking too much about big issues of existence such as what is the meaning of life. He went to Snowdonia in North Wales with his friends. One morning, he got up at dawn and decided to climb to the top of one of the peaks. He had thought about inviting his friends but felt he needed to do it alone. After an hour of climbing, when he reached the top of the peak, he experienced it in a way that he hadn't imagined.

He told me he perceived something deeply spiritual. His mind could not comprehend what he felt but he stood there in awe for some time. He touched something he later called *Immeasurable*. It embraced him and all things. He stayed up there for some hours abiding in this all-embracing Presence. John couldn't believe that such a thing could happen to him.

He came down from the peak. His friends noticed that he appeared different. They made a few jokes about him appearing like Moses, then they went off to the pub. From that moment John began reading what the prophets, saints and sages of past and present reported. He also regularly took long walks alone in nature.

There is a majesty to this perception of existence. It was the most important experience of John's life. One touch of such a deep experience can put so many of our other experiences into perspective, including our birth and death. However, we can't arrange for such experiences to arrive when we want them to – they come when the conditions are ripe.

In meditation, the perception of light and space can help overcome difficult states of mind. We can use light to overcome dark moods and perceptions of space to overcome heaviness. Moment to moment we let light into our eyes. We witness colours while keeping the body still. The eyeballs slowly move, attending to each colour. We cultivate the perception of space to overcome feelings of heaviness. We experience the space between objects, between sounds, and between thoughts. Perceptions change through altered states of consciousness or deep meditations. We have the potential to experience various perceptions apart from conventional ones. Clear perceptions, inner and outer, contribute to building our ability to see what matters and what doesn't.

Insight into the nature of things questions many commonly held perceptions. We perceive life free from the demands of self. We take care of what matters without becoming possessive. We perceive that ultimately nothing belongs to us. It never did. *I* have nothing to possess and *I* have nothing to lose – not in possessions, body, thoughts or feelings. *I* worry if I think *I* own anything. *I* then worry that *I* might lose everything. In truth *my* life does not belong to me but to the Nature of Things. This is the final aim of direct perception. The final understanding is liberating and enlightening.

INQUIRY

1. *What do you perceive as continuing?*

2. *Are you willing to change?*

3. *What do you hold fixed perceptions about?*

4. *Is the perception of yourself laced with negativity?*

5. *Have you had any deep experiences that have fundamentally altered your perceptions of what matters?*

Mental Formations, Thoughts

There is one thing that really matters to us: our state of mind. The formations of our mind are such an important feature of our lives, yet they rarely get the attention and interest that they deserve. Whatever we do and wherever we go, there is our state of mind. Body, feelings, perceptions, thoughts and consciousness mutually influence each other. Through awareness we can witness the arising and passing of the various formations of mind in the here and now. Thoughts act as the fuel for mental formations.

Feeling and perceptions give rise to thoughts. Thoughts create speech. Attitudes form. Beliefs arise. This sequence can then begin to create political, social and religious standpoints. Positions form in the individual and collective mind. These formations embrace power structures, hierarchical systems, the nation state, and countless divisions between people. The spark for conflicts springs from unexamined formations of mind.

In the Pali language the word for formations is *samkhara*. Etymologically, *samkhara* is a combination of two elements – *sam* means 'together' and *khara* means 'make'. It would appear that we spend our whole life under the influences of these formations. This places limits on how we see our relationship to existence. Through the depths of skilful meditation, mental formations quiet down without suppression. Wisdom and insight eradicate unsatisfactory formations.

Influential formations also arise from the forces of the past upon the present. This force is called 'karma'. Karmic formations influence perception and contribute to generating certain states of mind. The way thought moves into the future is also conditioned by these past forces playing on our mind. Every time our mind forms into such thought, it can trigger pressure. The thought formations then agitate and disturb our peace of mind. Waiting, worrying and thinking about the future becomes stressful. The desire to know an outcome fuels the thought and the thought fuels the desire. There is no rest or peace. It is not unusual for some people to be constantly in this mode of mind.

Karmic formations can arise in the guise of always wanting to be positive. Many people have a conditioned view that everything is getting better, and want to keep it that way. We resist hearing anything that questions that position. Remaining positive becomes a first priority. Others identify with the negative standpoint. Complaining, finding fault, constantly seeing what's wrong, becomes their pattern. There is a lack of trust in people and situations. The outcome is a dispirited attitude or cynicism.

Every year I travel to India. On the sixteen-hour train journey from New Delhi to Gaya in Bihar I once met a young Indian man named Rama. He said, 'It's OK for the Western tourists. They come for a few weeks or months on a cheap holiday to India. They return home with their experiences and photographs. They quickly forget our daily plight. We can't afford to go to the West. The West only wants our natural resources. Because some of us really want to go to the West, it makes us feel trapped in our own country.' There was some truth in what he said but what struck me most was the way his mind was running on from one demoralised thought to another.

Becoming aware of feelings, perceptions, thoughts, and mind-states, as well as outer formations, social and political, serves as a basis for insights into the way things arise from one another. In this process we can learn a great deal about ourselves. Thoughts show a primary formation of the mind. When well-established in meditation we can observe the gap between the thoughts. Such meditative observation helps to put the thoughts into perspective – to see a thought as a thought, no more, no less. This contributes to our understanding things in a completely different way.

We will discover much more in the silent space between thoughts than through all the interpretations, views and speculations that the formations of our mind generate. It then becomes clear to us that there is another way of knowing. We begin to trust in that space between thoughts and let ourselves sink deeply into it.

The realisation of the unformed, unmade and uncreated acts as the release from the formed, made and created. We see through this world of formations and its subsequent compounding of states of mind and matter. The formations fit into the nature of things like waves in the ocean. All is water. They belong to that which is indestructible. When one has realised this there is an immeasurable freedom in knowing intuitively the unformed.

PRACTICE

1. You are sitting in a café drinking a cup of coffee. A man sits alone at a nearby table. He is looking rather pensive. You barely notice him. There is just his physical formation; you carry on reading. Suddenly this young man puts his head in his hands and starts crying. Do you watch your thoughts? Feel irritated? Let your thoughts speculate? Send him feelings of loving kindness? Or walk over and gently ask him if there is anything you can do?

2. What are the unsatisfactory states of mind that you can change?

3. Can you see a thought just as a thought? Notice the way perceptions and feelings form thoughts, and thoughts become an attitude.

4. If what has formed is a problem, to dissolve it requires insight. Bring full awareness to bear on these formations until insights make the difference. What is the insight that makes the difference?

5. Meditate on the Unformed – even if it sounds vague and abstract. The key to this meditation is calm awareness of utter silence and stillness of being.

Consciousness

The word *consciousness* is not necessarily easy to understand since we use it in so many different ways. Theologians, scholars and philosophers give the concept all sorts of sophisticated meanings that can end up leaving us baffled. In this text, consciousness has a simple meaning. It means 'to be conscious of'. I call mindfulness an energised consciousness.

The burglar tiptoeing across the bedroom is extraordinarily mindful every time his foot touches the ground or he hears a sound in the rest of the house. Single-pointed focus, interest and energy heighten his consciousness. The quality of his mindfulness is moment-to-moment – a quality that most meditators would envy. However, the burglar lacks clear comprehension of the suffering he generates. He ignores the selfishness of his intentions and the consequences of his actions – a gross mind supporting a gross conscious.

Sometimes we are barely conscious. We walk down the street.

We are sufficiently conscious to get from A to B but hardly observe or notice our environment due to our involvement in fantasies, daydreams and wandering thoughts. If we are not sufficiently mindful we bump into people, sprain an ankle or get lost.

Since it means 'conscious of', consciousness acts as the subject and reveals the objects, including the condition of mind. We can be clearly conscious of feelings, moods, thoughts, states of mind, body and sense objects. We are not what we can be conscious of. When the condition of our consciousness is not flitting from one thing to another we see situations much more clearly. We can experience the benefit of a steady consciousness. Clinging to objects, internal and external, pushes and pulls our consciousness around. We are then completely at the mercy of objects of interest that enter influence and give shape to consciousness.

Energised with clear comprehension, consciousness beneficially influences our state of mind concerning past, present or future. Through clear comprehension we understand what causes suffering and what resolves it. Old formations, attitudes and tendencies then have less influence on consciousness. We can experience clear interaction with the world when not weighed down with habits and addictions glued to consciousness.

A television programme reported the case of the diligent psychotherapist who spent thousands of hours working with hardened, violent men in the prison system. Many of them had killed for the sake of killing, without feeling any remorse. They murdered as a result of a minor disagreement or purely for the lust of it. The psychotherapist got to know them, and made a video of some of his meetings with them. As they established trust and confidence in him, the killers began to talk about their childhood – the physical and sexual abuse which had often occurred over long periods of time. These men had learnt at a vulnerable age that living meant abusing and violating.

Some of the men began to touch their childhood experiences and their 'frozen terror', as the psychotherapist called it. This meant that their consciousness became beneficially exposed to the unresolved pressures from the past. These problems included fear, hate, disgust and rage against life. As they unfroze their pain, by becoming conscious of these emotions, their views towards themselves and others began to change. In some cases the psychotherapist became confident enough to speak of cures.

Whether in gross or subtle aspects, the past can cast its shadow over consciousness. We think we know what we are seeing in front of us. We often fail to acknowledge that what we see is mostly the state of our mind. When consciousness is under the influence of the past, it is like looking at the world with coloured sunglasses. We may see darkness everywhere.

The influences from the past, which can be wholesome or unwholesome, can lead us towards painful realms of experience. We often maintain that only evil acts can take us to hell, i.e. degrees of suffering that are overwhelming. That is not necessarily the case. The force of the wholesome can be under the spell of ignorance, and consciousness is then pushed into hell. For example, we are doing good. We get very attached to doing good. We want to do more and more. We put immense pressure on ourselves. We get very dependent on achieving the results that we set ourselves. Then it all goes wrong. We end up in hell. Burnt out. A nervous breakdown. Devastated with feelings of worthlessness. Energetic collapse; emotional despair; bodily exhaustion. Or worse.

PRACTICE

1. *What habits and patterns sow the seeds for the most suffering?*

2. *What changes are you willing to make?*

3. *Initiate one of these changes on a regular basis.*

4. *Acknowledge to yourself and others the benefit of making such a change.*

A young woman knew she had to bring her consciousness to bear on a particular problem. She had to get over her fear of expressing a different point of view when talking to others. Whenever there was a group discussion at work she remained quiet. She was afraid that if she spoke her mind there might be a backlash, so she preferred to keep quiet. Inwardly, she could not keep quiet. Her mind would not let her. Negative or resentful thoughts would emerge from within towards herself and others. She also held back from expressing warmth and tenderness to others in case they misunderstood her. She realised she could not go on like this and decided that:

1. She would voice a concern or criticism to somebody once every five days.

2. She would express words of appreciation to somebody for who they were and what they did.

3. She would continue to tell a close friend what she was doing until the confidence to speak her heart and mind got established.

As a result, over several months, she grew in confidence about expressing her own views and her resentment faded.

It is this process of becoming fully conscious of our state of mind that makes such a difference to our lives. We have evolved in the material and scientific world to an alarming degree but we have not addressed the evolution of consciousness fully enough. The practice of evolving our consciousness comes through insight, clear comprehension, and diminishing those unhealthy patterns that affect every area of our lives. Not surprisingly, psychotherapy and mind-body workers have replaced priests as guiding lights. Unresolved issues from childhood have replaced original sin. The karma of the past (that means something unsatisfactory from the past influencing the present) can dissolve. The teachings point to the liberation of consciousness from entrapment in unsatisfactory mental states.

INQUIRY

1. *Consciousness can run up and down between the three fields of time – past, present and future – or get established in the here and now. What is your priority?*

2. *In which area(s) do you need to raise your level of consciousness?*

3. *What do you need to direct consciousness towards?*

4. *In an expanded consciousness, what do you sense?*

FIVE HINDRANCES

Fixed thoughts are relentlessly punishing.
So why hide behind our loutish intellect?
Putting aside this cruel pretence
Of civilisation amid our broken toys,
Let us pay respect to this awareness.

Introduction

Each of the Hindrances – sense desire, anger, boredom, restless-ness and doubt – beset human existence with all of their painful consequences. No one is more or less acceptable than the others.

Dharma teachings employ practices, dialogue and meditation for insight into the Hindrances. This understanding is not an intel-lectual understanding about the causes of any of the Hindrances. Insight serves only to reduce or eliminate the force of a Hindrance.

We practise to see into the beliefs and motivations that support a Hindrance. We keep alive our resolve to overcome them. We either attend directly to the Hindrance itself, or deepen our medi-tation so that the Hindrance collapses through lack of support.

At times awareness of the general circumstances of our daily life becomes a key factor to resolve the Hindrances. Looking at each of them, we may become aware that one or more stands out. We take note of this and find and develop skilful ways, including the necessary effort, to overcome the Hindrances. Depths of medita-tion, insight and changes in our life can resolve any of them.

There is a commonly held view that we all have all Five Hindrances to a greater or lesser extent throughout our lives. The teachings challenge this view. We have the potential to live a ful-filled life free from even temporary imprisonment in these Hindrances. One significant understanding can alter the various formations and constructions in our inner life, causing a Hindrance to collapse. What was once a problem ceases to be one. We need to stay committed to finding a wise resolution. When we keep telling ourselves we have such a big problem or addiction to overcome, we easily get overwhelmed. It is doing something skilful about the problem that counts. Happiness and contentment are among the fruits of such practices. Ceasing to feed Hindrances brings its own joy.

Sense Desire

Wishing to impress shareholders, the chairman of Coca-Cola told them at the annual general meeting:

A billion hours ago life appeared on earth.

A billion minutes ago Christianity emerged.

A billion seconds ago the Beatles changed music for ever.

A billion Coca-Colas ago was yesterday morning.

To become chairman of Coca-Cola, arguably the world's most famous brand name, ranks as a remarkable achievement in the corporate world. The chairman must have extraordinary skills in management, marketing and communication. The thought arose in my mind, 'I wonder if the Coca-Cola chairman ever felt it to be a pity that he placed his considerable expertise, as well as devoting much of his life, to promoting an artificial drink.' I wish he had told shareholders he had had a billion thoughts that day about it!

We live in a culture that works incessantly trying to satisfy every imaginable desire for every sense door. We all know that differences in colour, taste or whatever are utterly inconsequential but we quickly forget. So we end up getting caught in numerous desires to get what we want. It makes life hard for the producers, hard for the employees and hard for the customers. There is constant pressure on everybody to make as much money as possible in the forlorn hope that it will make our lives content, happy and fulfilled. Working incredibly hard to maximise income, indulgent shopping sprees and the endless pursuit of pleasure thrive on unexamined beliefs. This constant pursuit of self-gratification springs from joylessness. When things go wrong, worry, resentment and selfish demands fill the mind.

Trapped in the forces of wanting and hating, the mind lives in a deluded condition. Life becomes just the producing and consuming of goods and services. There may be little real awareness of anything else except the state of personal relationships. These inner distortions become so widespread that few question this state of mental dis-ease.

This addiction to pleasure through the senses becomes a way of life. Something new, something old, something different: there is a pull towards constantly changing what comes to our senses. We get tired of one thing so we move on to something else. We seem to be afraid of questioning this thirst for pleasure. Instead of trying to shed light on enlightenment, we opt instead for a way of life that is a blight on enlightenment. The allure of pleasure mesmerises the mind. We can never satisfy the mind's desire for things for very long. We even make selfish desire a virtue rather than a severe problematic hindrance to love, integrity and wisdom.

Caught up in a world of projections, we fantasise what it would be like to be rich, to do what we liked if we only had the money. Despite years of work, most homes are not flooded with expensive goods. In the excesses of our imagination, in indulging in fantasy, we breed discontent within. We may not realise how blessed we are to be free from opulence and ostentatious living among people who constantly need their egos pampered.

We like to rationalise this magnetic pull to the daily pursuit of more pleasure and profit through belief in choice. If this is our choice, then our thirst for more seems to force us to choose anger, boredom, anxiety and self-doubt. It takes practice, right effort and clarity to work towards liberation from obstacles to a well-integrated life.

Some people live just to pay off their debts. Credit and loans can generate financial imprisonment. Banks, loan companies and business encourage the 'live now, pay later' view of existence. More and more students find themselves in debt. Some governments allow students to run up large debts to pay for their education. Having submitted to the pressures of university life, graduates then join a company only to spend years paying off their debts. Such debts become a contemporary form of bonded labour.

Unless there is financial prudence, debts can produce despair and conflict for the individual and family. The cost of indulging one reckless desire can be daily misery. The exchange of money is as much of an emotional transaction as a simple statement of figures. Unresolved issues around money produce worry, anger and fear. It is not that many people are greedy, even when they overeat, but they might be anxious and insecure. Constant struggles to keep weight down often reflect unhappiness and agitation in a person's emotional life. 'I am digging my grave with a knife and fork,' said one overweight woman. We deceive ourselves if we think we will be better off through *having* rather than through insight and wisdom.

Occasionally, the public voice of criticism against the kings and queens of hedonism and the fat cats triggers moral shame in some of them. However, there is no substitute for the honest self-examination which often marks the beginning of real inner change. Wisdom reveals a non-greedy and unselfish way of being in this world.

PRACTICE

1. *Do you have the strength of mind to keep clear from debts?*

2. *Do you experience peace with what is or are you constantly thinking about and working for what you want?*

3. *Can this feeling of never having enough be satisfied with income and goods?*

4. *Do you own possessions or do they own you?*

5. *What fills you with appreciative joy unrelated to goods, money and personal success?*

6. *What is the greatest obstruction to a liberated life?*

Anger

I pulled into a local car park, spotted a space, and drove into it. I hadn't noticed that the car in front of me was moving slowly forward to reverse into the same space. The driver of the car, a huge thug of a man, strode up to me and said, 'Get your fucking car out of that spot.' I told the man I had not realised that he intended to go into reverse. He cursed me again. So I added: 'I am not going to move my car one inch through being sworn at by you.' He then got very angry. 'If you don't get your fucking car out of there I'm going to smash your face in.' It was showdown time!

Standing eyeball to eyeball, toe to toe, I said: 'I told you. I won't move until you drop your threat. Not one inch.' He was breathing heavily. He lifted up a clenched fist. A few people began watching the incident. And then he said with concealed fury: 'Please move your car.' I said, 'Thank you,' got in my car and reversed out. One never gets any satisfaction (well, maybe a little) from standing one's ground. Such anger may spill over on to somebody else, more vulnerable than me. Yet we must be prepared to dig our heels in and say no to aggression. We must find the strength of mind to take the consequences on a point of principle.

Anger often becomes the outer expression of different kinds of state of mind. Among the triggers for anger are:

1. Not getting what we want. The investment in and desire to get what we want builds up a dependency. When our demands are not forthcoming we get angry – with others, with ourselves. Or there can be bitter disappointment over the outcome, then a short time later we get angry over the most trivial thing. Instead of dumping the anger on the primary object of interest, it finds its outlet on a secondary area of attention.

2. Feeling hurt and then getting angry. Unable to handle feelings of rejection and emotional hurt, we get upset and inflamed by what a person has said or done to us. This anger is a type of frustration, leaving us under the influence of another.

3. Being afraid and attacking back in rage. We have probably seen a dog cowering in a corner when under attack. It goes from fear to attacking back and then back to fear. In the same way we can go back and forth between fear and rage. Under the influence of the instinct for flight or fight, we find ourselves in turmoil.

4. Feelings of helplessness triggered by current circumstances. Some people are afraid to speak up or challenge a view different from their own. They hold back. This becomes a pattern. Later it manifests as constantly complaining about others behind their backs, blame, and cynicism.

5. Frozen emotional life, sometimes due to childhood abuse. Acts of violence become the learned form of contact with others. Violent men and women often have a history of exposure to violence from childhood or have learnt it, perhaps in the armed forces. Unable to deal with the forces of conditioning, they live out their rage and anger against others. Under the influence of intense pressure, alcohol and drugs, violence may erupt despite a healthy childhood upbringing. In those attracted to notoriety, obedience, power and weapons, the mind can become violent.

Anger generates heat from within burning us up. But it also becomes a pattern. We imagine that we can control others through getting angry with them, but what we generate is resentment. Anger is not only ugly and potentially destructive, but also a very poor strategy for dealing with problems. Advice only works when the person shows real motivation to change. Otherwise the words go in one ear and out of the other. Realising that the self is not really different from the self of another helps dissolve explosive anger and lingering hostility.

This insight is elucidated by two boys who were playing with a little girl's ball. She wanted the ball back. They refused to give it. She started crying, so they began to tease her. She began to yell and scream at them. They continued to play their game in a more exaggerated way, becoming more arrogant and bullying. This situation happens frequently between nations, rulers and ruled, parents and children, religious authorities and followers. The ball becomes the metaphor for something both sides want, but for one to receive it, the other has to let go since the self is not at a deeper level different from the other.

There is also the all-too-human aspect of anger. A father was waiting for his sixteen-year-old daughter to come home late one Saturday night. She had been out clubbing with her friends. He had said that she had to be back by 12.30 a.m. At 12.45 a.m. she had not returned. Thirty minutes later she still had not returned home. From 1 a.m. he kept pulling aside the curtained window to look up and down the street. His mind began to worry. He felt the pressure of his anger inside. He found the thought forming in his mind of what he would say to her when she got in. He began thinking of the way he would punish her.

When she walked in, she made a short apology and zoomed

upstairs to her room, not wanting to hear her father's wrath. Suddenly, he remembered that when he was young he had done the same to his parents. He was relieved she was home safe and sound. He went upstairs and spoke to her quietly and supportively for a few minutes. She agreed she would make every effort in future to be home on time, or at least ring if there was some delay. He realised how close he had come to getting into a rage. Was the fact that she was an hour late the problem? Was it that he could not control her life? Anger does not control others. It makes them resentful. It takes motivation, co-operation and mutual understanding to transform the mind.

PRACTICE

1. *In anger and revenge, we sink to the level of others. It is also our mind that burns and suffers. Develop noble silence rather than support unhealthy attitudes.*

2. *Practise letting go of any negativities that infect your memory.*

3. *If sending an aggressive letter, practise waiting overnight before posting it.*

4. *Practise resisting the temptation to justify negativity.*

5. *Explore a wise response to others' behaviour.*

6. *Reflect on what stands beyond getting or not getting your own way.*

Boredom and Apathy

Boredom besieges all ages and we stimulate our senses in order to overcome it. As a result, we have become beggars at the sense doors and slaves to the endless pursuit of pleasurable sensations through our eyes, ears, nose, tongue and touch to relieve the way we slug along in everyday life. We imagine the whole reason for existence is maximising the number of pleasurable experiences and minimising the unpleasant ones. Yet making this our primary aim actually invites countless unpleasant states of mind and we eventually get bored with this pursuit too. Boredom takes natural enjoyment out of everyday events, even though enjoyment of life is our birthright.

Boredom may be the outcome of disappointment, isolation, unresolved anger, excessive familiarity with the immediate environment, or identification with periods of low energy. In the grip of our boredom we move rather sluggishly from one activity to another. Withdrawal or irritability are close companions of boredom and apathy.

Constantly watching television reveals one of the greatest demonstrations of indifference to the real world. The cynically clever television advertisements in the USA say: 'It's a beautiful day outside. Why aren't you at home watching television?' We watch one television programme after another with boredom. Habituated to the *on* switch, we have no power left to use the *off* switch. Boredom manifests through inactivity and activity. Without gossip, without talking behind people's backs, there would even be greater levels of boredom.

We get bored because we:

1. Are reluctant to change habitual patterns.
2. Can't perceive challenges.
3. Abuse alcohol and drugs.
4. Lack appreciation for the ordinary.
5. Use boredom to cover up anger.
6. Fear taking risks.

Boredom certainly deserves the same kind of care and attention we give to the other Hindrances. The boredom we feel also has its impact on the lives of others and on our environment. It can become pathological. If it does, no fresh pleasurable sensations can break its spell. Pervasive boredom will manifest as compulsive needs for alcohol, cigarettes, gambling, making money, and forever moaning.

Marcus and Sylvia had been in a relationship for several months. They were not living together but were getting closer to doing so. One day at his flat she saw his telephone bill, which came to several hundred pounds. She noticed that nearly all of the bill referred to one particular number. Her first thought was *another woman*. She looked at the number and saw that it was not a private number but a public one: he was spending a fortune on a sex line.

She was shocked. Some of the calls he made were on the same evening that he had spoken to her. 'He must find me incredibly boring,' she thought. But then she realised that he was the one who had the problem, and she eased herself out of the relationship. It is in this state of something lacking, something missing, that the mind pursues an outlet to overcome that hole inside. It can often become a secret life, hidden from our loved ones. Relief of boredom is easily exploited and can be extraordinarily expensive.

We deceive ourselves if we think busyness resolves boredom. Busyness exhausts us, making us even more vulnerable to boredom. Boredom weighs on consciousness. It is only a matter of degree before it becomes depression. Squeezing the life out of us, it inhibits our capacity to respond fully to situations. As it encroaches on our existence, we experience the loss of vitality in our cells. Our posture slumps. We turn restlessly from side to side or stare aimlessly, not knowing what to do with ourselves. The resolution requires creative initiatives, but that's easier said than done.

Pierre had worked incredibly hard, far too many hours in the day. He hated his job and all the pressure that went with it. He started to notice a lingering state of tiredness. He not only felt bored with his life, but the lack of enthusiasm was draining too. He thought it was a passing phase, only to find it did not go away. As time went by, it became more and more of a struggle to get himself out of bed in the morning. He realised that his body was in the process of adapting to his general state of mind. Fortunately, he had enough determination left to get out of his field of work before it was too late. After a time, he found renewal. But others are not always so fortunate.

It is common enough knowledge that living without awareness generates dullness as a side effect, Any attachment to gross, pleasurable sensations also has its consequence. We need more than pursuit of pleasure in life to prevent boredom from weighing down the mind. We need the practice of developing our consciousness to go from gross desires to subtle appreciations in daily life. If it were our last day on earth would we feel bored? The grip of boredom takes away appreciation and love for the ordinary. The connection with the new day, the enjoyment of a momentary meeting, and the refusal to live in the shadow of mindless repetition safeguards us from a slide into apathy.

There is something suffocating about being immersed in the sea of pleasure. The inner life becomes stifled with such sensations. When the sensations fade, as they do, we feel empty and unhappy. When all of that drops away, when the curtain has fallen, when we return home to our ordinary sense of self, it can be devastating. We forget that the inflation of the self is the invitation to its deflation. We may not even know what we want, yet there is no doubt we get what we deserve.

INQUIRY

1. *Imagine it is your last day on earth. You have no tomorrow, no future. You can't do anything wild or insensitive.*
2. *How would you spend your last day?*
3. *What would you give attention to?*
4. *What would you take time to observe?*
5. *What would you appreciate or reflect upon?*
6. *Now go ahead and do it before it is your last day!*

Restlessness and Worry

There is much pressure upon us all to conform. People get plaudits for living in the same house, keeping the same job, and continuing for a long time in the same relationship. These are seen as signs of stability. There are others who express a different way of being in the world. Not for them the same home, the same job, the same friends. They are a generation of people who prefer to be on the move. They live in a world of change; and their outer life expresses it.

Others suddenly become restless. On impulse they grasp an idea without awareness of the consequences. Sometimes the outcome is foolhardy, creating unnecessary anguish, and sometimes the outcome is simply eccentric, as in the following case. A resident of Los Angeles named Larry was feeling restless and decided to float thirty feet above his home. He went to the local Army-Navy surplus store and bought forty-five weather balloons and several tanks of helium. He tied a chair to his jeep, attached the helium-filled balloons to the chair, and sat down on it. He then cut the ropes holding the chair down. In his lap he had a pellet gun to puncture the balloons one by one, so he could float gently down again on to his back garden. Instead of floating lazily up to thirty feet, however, Larry soared straight up to a height of 11,000 feet. He drifted for fourteen hours until spotted by the crew of a passenger plane. The pilot reported to air traffic control that he had seen a man sitting in a chair at 11,000 feet, moving slowly (and helplessly) towards Los Angeles International Airport. Eventually a helicopter rescued Larry out over the ocean, and the police arrested him for violating air space.

It is all too easy for those who show outer stability to criticise those who make frequent changes in their lives. They will say, 'Isn't it about time that you settled down?' We are arrogant when we inflict this view on everybody who lives differently from the conventional forms. Restlessness has nothing intrinsically to do with whether we move a lot or not. The outer expression of our life does not give an accurate reflection of our inner life. Restlessness can pervade both outer and inner life and be a major hindrance to enlightenment.

We need to know ourselves. This includes learning to observe our reactions and developing the skills to handle things that upset us. When restlessness enters deeply into our emotional life, it triggers worry, fear and panic. We harass ourselves over matters of past, present and future. We begin thinking exclusively in terms of cause and effect.

Restlessness and worry mark a clear signal that we have become terribly caught up in our cause-effect thinking. Worry reveals unsettled feelings and thoughts about the past, present and future. We worry for ourselves and we worry for others. Nobody benefits from worry. We have to be very clear about that. It's a service to all to bring our mind back to the present moment, breathe in and out firmly, so that we clear out the stressful thinking. Later we might say, 'Well I was right after all. I really had something to worry about.' We then forget that worry only reveals the tendency to fret over situations, a lack of inner steadiness. It shows unskilful dramatisation of a situation.

The direct way to avoid worry is regular meditation and

attending to the whole process of inner events. This process might include tracking your relationship to memory, perceptions, feelings and thoughts, and observing what they make of past, present and future. You might notice any thoughts about the thoughts. This additional flow of thoughts may help to clarify or add turmoil. This reduces the blind tendency to identify with everything, to make a problem out of everything. Learning to track the process takes the drama out of the movement. You could keep a journal exploring ways to handle events with clarity.

We may be given advice on how to cope with worry but we may not want to let go of our view, no matter how distressing it is. We believe in our position, cling to it, even though we ask others for their perception of the situation.

What are some of the ways that we can work with such a situation?

PRACTICE

1. *Remember to breathe to dispel and soften the obsessive thinking.*

2. *Develop the capacity to take steps to resolve a problem.*

3. *Recognise what is supportive from others.*

4. *Practise letting go of the words of others who want to put you down.*

5. *Develop skilful action rather than look for approval.*

6. *Practise recognising useful criticism from others.*

Carlos was a divorced man in his early fifties, Ingrid, his partner, was in her twenties. She had been reluctant to go with him to the annual dinner for architects in a European city. The thought of it made her restless. She had no appetite for the meat dishes, the after-dinner speeches, the small talk and the clouds of cigar smoke polluting the air. Against her better judgement, she agreed to go. Halfway through dinner a middle-aged woman sitting opposite Ingrid and Carlos turned to her husband and said: 'That [Ingrid] is his mattress', implying that Carlos only wanted Ingrid for sex.

The remark inflamed the young woman. She turned to Carlos, who had also heard the remark, but he said nothing, not a word, and carried on eating. The attitude of the middle-aged woman and Carlos's silence left Ingrid upset and angry. She felt agitated and humiliated throughout the meal, and vowed she would never again go to such a function. For a long time afterwards she felt disappointed with her partner for keeping his mouth shut.

We never know what remarks will get flung at us, privately or publicly. We can get more agitated with friends who keep a stiff upper lip than with people who make hurtful remarks. Feeling hurt and agitated is no resolution. It can be an act of personal responsibility to speak up for ourselves rather than waiting around for others to do so. Ingrid might have told the woman what she though of her, but she didn't.

When we experience restlessness, painful movements of the mind, or conflicts of decisions, we feel very unsteady. It is like being out at the end of a branch, and blown backwards and forwards. The more we think, the more unsettled we become. We need to remember to breathe in and out mindfully, to write out our restlessness, to express ourselves through dance and movement. The dissolution of the restlessness about yesterday and today and the anxiety about tomorrow brings us closer to seeing things clearly. When we know the truth of the matter, we can stay steady with the truth; we find a true place of rest. To attend to the truth rather than fight it, brings peace.

INQUIRY

1. *What are the core beliefs in your restlessness?*
2. *Do you really want to stop worrying?*
3. *What is neglected in worry?*
4. *Worry is not a proof of love. What is?*
5. *What can you discover before thoughts arise?*

Doubt

Doubts can arise around any issue of importance. The attention focuses around a particular person or thing. In that relationship, the mind moves backwards and forwards not knowing whether to act or not. The mind torments itself. In the instability of such a situation, you find yourself seeking a solution from friends. Their views can vary considerably as well, which only contributes further to feeding the doubt. It can become chronic.

We have the capacity to think a great deal about something or someone who matters to us. We can make ourselves feel ill through so much thinking. When our mind runs around and around, we experience doubt, fear and confusion. One part of the mind struggles with another part of the mind for supremacy. We don't know who or what to believe. Healers tell us to listen to our inner voice. But what do we do when we hear more than one inner voice? We can go to bed convinced of one position and wake up in the morning convinced of the opposite standpoint.

We imagine that doubts and indecision affect perhaps one or two areas of our life. It is rarely the case. We can have the same state of mind when buying an inexpensive consumer item, making a minor telephone call or eating an extra mouthful of food. If we learn to act clearly and firmly in minor situations, this gives us the training for handling major issues.

We often give too much weight to our thoughts. The more we think, the more confused we feel. Self-doubt then acts like a virus. It doesn't seem to do us or anyone any good whatsoever. Dharma teachings, the practices of mindfulness, unwavering focus and resolution enable us to drop the excesses of our thinking. Bereft of contradictory standpoints through the practice of minimising thinking, we can see our way clear. The practice of meditation and applying mindfulness to daily life contributes to reducing the inner forces of indecision and contradictory attitudes. Breathing methods and keeping resolutions help stabilise the mind.

We can only act in response to what we know and understand. It takes a degree of trust and faith in ourselves. There is the danger that our ego will feed ruthlessly upon our decisions, boosting us up or putting us down. This will increase the intensity of doubts if things go wrong. It is little comfort to know that countless others are in the same plight.

Someone acting as a support to a person dying at home from AIDS rang me to say that the patient was experiencing doubts about the ethics of intentionally bringing his life to a close. He was not so much afraid of death but of acting unwisely in facing the biggest challenge of all – reaching the end of his existence. With the complete breakdown of his immune system, the cancer in his body had spread to his brain. He wished to die as mindfully as possible. The patient wanted to know my thoughts on taking a lethal dosage in such circumstances. What was worse? To choose to continue in this terrible state of mental and physical deterioration or to act while the mind was relatively clear? I said that I needed to speak to the patient, whom I had known for seventeen years. He was so weak he could not hear my voice on the phone. At the request of his support group, I left my comments on his answering machine. They then turned the volume up for him to hear. He listened several times. All this occurred late in the morning; that evening the dying person overdosed his medication and immediately passed out of this world. Who has the right to comment on matters of life and death? Who has the right to take a position? Who is qualified? We perceive a situation and we respond to it.

Doubts also arise for those deeply committed to the spiritual life and religion. A woman had been very devoted to her spiritual teacher for years. She had followed him around the world. Then a doubt began to enter her mind. He claimed enlightenment but she frequently saw him bullying a number of his followers. He kept boasting that he was free and abided in Oneness, but needed bodyguards to protect him – although nobody gave him a second thought outside his group. He felt a compelling need to see the faults of others and rubbish them publicly and privately.

She kept thinking to herself 'If he is free, what does he have to be afraid of?' Freedom from fear is a fundamental freedom. Her doubts began to grow. This group and the teacher had absorbed her whole life. Since she had nowhere to turn, she could only live with the group in a submissive capacity. Secretly she feared she had been cultivating emotional clinging. This kind of doubt can be useful. It forces us to question our attachment and cherished views. There is doubt that is a hindrance to our development and doubt that contributes to it. Insight reveals the difference between them.

There are those who stick tenaciously to one teacher, tradition, book or form. It becomes a means for attachment and inevitably restricts authentic freedom. There are others who go from one thing to another – the spiritual supermarket mentality. They constantly hunt for new experiences. This can lend itself to a superficial understanding of things, with doubts inevitably arising. It is still ego, whether it is the ego of narrow mindedness or the ego of broad mindedness. When grounded in the Threefold Training, a commitment to one avenue of exploration or to more than one is secondary. Morality, depths of awareness and wisdom come first. The direct way to deal with persistent and troublesome doubts is to mindfully breathe through thoughts, and practise staying steady with morality, awareness training and meditation. If there are still doubts, then seek the wisdom of those free from doubts, confusion and clinging.

INQUIRY

1. *Doubts can be healthy whether born from inquiry or confusion. What shows the difference?*

2. *When your mind is uncertain, what determines a decision?*

3. *Certain doubts act as a hindrance. Hindrance to what?*

4. *Is it wise or foolish to act under pressure?*

5. *What embraces all faith and doubts?*

THREE
CHARACTERISTICS
OF EXISTENCE

We know little of who we are; but our self
Is rooted in measurement,
Strange and thought-driven.
Limited by circumstances, but refusing to admit;
Functional, irregular; a claimer of experiences.

Introduction

The three characteristics of existence are impermanence, suffering (including dissatisfaction) and not-self. To meditate directly on these Three Characteristics provides insights. It is the inability to understand and accommodate the presence of these Characteristics that makes life for humanity so difficult. However, we need to remember they are Characteristics of *Existence*, not the ultimate truth.

How much unhappiness and grief have we experienced through our inability to understand change, pain and ego-identification? How much dissatisfaction do we experience through the interactivity of feelings, perceptions, thoughts, memories and stories? Yet we identify ourselves with the first two Characteristics of Existence as though they were the supreme reality of a real self. Awareness of life as a process helps reveal the not-self of it all.

The sense of *I* easily becomes entangled in the field of mind-body. We think that we conceive and produce all of our states of mind. The mind-body belongs to a moment to moment process, not to self. It is an error of perception to assume that there is a permanent *I* that lords over the mind and body. Pure witnessing of mind-body gives the opportunity for insights into the process.

We live in a world of change so we get easily caught up in the satisfaction-dissatisfaction cycle. We then think of the dependently arising conditions of mind-body as self, as me, as who I am. Pure witnessing of this process of mind-body changes this possessive thought. There is an understanding in terms of process rather than claims of the ego.

Direct and sustained witnessing of the three characteristics contribute to clarity in the mind. We then have the potential to know a grounded and emancipated life. Insight into these characteristics arise through experience, meditation, reflection and inquiry.

Impermanence

I arrived in India in 1967. I was a young man in my early twenties, and had travelled overland from Britain. Just outside Varanasi is the village of Sarnath, the place where the Buddha gave his first talk. On a table in one of the temples there was an array of small books on the teachings of the Buddha. I picked up two of them, briefly thumbed through them, and bought both since they gave teachings on the Four Noble Truths, the Noble Eightfold Path, and so on.

At that time, two features of the teachings stood out significantly. The Buddha reminded people frequently that *all conditioned things are impermanent.* Secondly, since everything is impermanent, *nothing is worth clinging to.* I took the impermanence and non-clinging discussed in those small books very much to heart. These two points acted as a tremendous support as I continued my travels. It is the inner experience of the truth of things that makes the difference. I gradually began to realise the wisdom and the honesty required to stay steady with such basic realities of everyday life, and wanted to spend more time investigating them. Three years later I became a Buddhist monk.

We would not waste a moment of our time if we contemplated change and investigated through our experience the way things affect and condition each other. Out of such authentic perceptions we would realise the uselessness of any form of clinging and holding. Such experiences and insights would not bring a withdrawal from the world but would contribute significantly to a clearer insight into the way things are. We would continue our journey in accordance with day-to-day life rather than living in the shadow of the unclear self.

The diversity of things becomes apparent when we keep our eyes, ears and mind open. The sheer scale, if not grandeur, of all of this manifests itself through our senses day in and day out. Yet every contact, every item, every impression is subject to arising and passing. Consciousness moves in association with this world of contact. We take a few things out of all this diversity and fuel their significance. Some things then matter in our lives more than other things. All of this is natural and appropriate.

If we give unwise attention to various features of life, inner and outer, we suffer. It means that we have lost touch with impermanence and substituted clinging in an area of life that we have highlighted. This is due to a shift in emphasis occurring in the deeply rooted feeling of *I*. The *I* gets embedded with a sticky quality. We begin to glue our self around the perception or impression of the object, including mind and body.

We identify with these impressions. The *I* gains a substantiality, and so does what it has fastened upon. In reality neither possess such a characteristic. When our self grasps experiences, ideas, situations and people, we get exposed to troublesome mind-states. We get caught up in things changing or not seeming to change. Lacking wisdom, we fall back on to the condition of the *I* and the history of its relationship with the object. We may experience hurt, sadness, anger, disappointment and anxiety due to the form of accumulated dependency. We may fuel fresh desires and go off at tangents. A range of mind-states cling together due to this stickiness in *I* and *my*. Practice dissolves the stickiness in *I* and *my*.

In the insight meditation tradition there is a great deal of emphasis on learning to witness impermanence from moment to moment. It is easy to engage in the language of *everything is impermanent*. It is something else to feel it in our bones. Such understanding may come temporarily through sudden changes of circumstances, but that does not mean it will be a sustainable and constant awareness. That comes with depth of wisdom and clarity.

The world of change reveals itself exclusively through the field of objects – objects of the eye, ear, nose, tongue, touch, and objects in the mind that relate to past, present and future. Impermanence does not exist outside the field of objects. We know therefore what we have to deal with. When we cling to any of these objects, we will suffer sooner or later.

Those things that we love can bring us a great deal of happiness and joy in life, but without wisdom we will suffer uselessly and naively over change. Suffering does not arise from love as we commonly like to believe, nor is it a proof of love. It springs from the clinging self. Suffering arises through lack of wisdom and understanding. For those to be present requires a depth of awareness and a love far greater than living in dependency.

We live in a world of multiple and diverse objects, many of which have very little impact upon us. We remember only some of the things that happen to us. Whatever we select is tiny compared with what daily life exposes us to. To suffer over impermanence is to live under a spell of unclarity, and our consciousness becomes restricted. If we break out of this spell, we realise a free life respectful of change.

It is not unusual for some authority, whether in science, philosophy or religion, to make the claim that impermanence is the ultimate truth. This view gives substantial reality to the appearance of conditioned objects and awards them a status that is greater than their individual merit. Dispensing with such views, we simply experience the arising and passing of objects of attention. Yet we do not make witnessing impermanence an end in itself.

Genuine awareness of change reduces the anguish that can besiege our lives. This means we shift away from objects, things and the indulgence of mind in the impermanent. It awakens us to something greater; we have a different sense and yearning, taking us in a new direction. There is no real contentment with the changeable. Death ends the association with the changeable. So it would seem wise and skilful to turn our attention from the measurable to the Immeasurable that embraces birth and death.

We are used to thinking about things lasting and not lasting. We acknowledge that everything exists for a period of time and then stops existing. Circumstances arise and pass, come and go. Every experience, every thought, every contact and every relationship become subject to change. Impermanence is a feature of moment-to-moment life. When we neglect these simple, everyday relative truths, we can get angry or sad. To witness impermanence and to reflect on it daily is a sign of wisdom.

One of the significant factors about sustained awareness of change and impermanence is the impact that it has on our perceptions. Realising the emptiness of craving for the changeable sets us free. We are no longer stuck with the world of the conditioned and the fear of death that cuts us off from it. Dissolving our clinging around what is impermanent exposes that beyond the measurable.

PRACTICE

1. *Be mindful of change, of arising and passing.*

2. *Observe the effect of healthy and unhealthy attitudes towards change.*

3. *Notice the way the satisfactory becomes the unsatisfactory and vice versa.*

4. *Meditate on the question, 'Is there a release from living in change?'*

In formal meditation, we can intentionally observe changes from one moment to the next in the breath, body sensations, feelings, thoughts and sounds as they come and go. This is what it means to witness impermanence. A breath comes and it goes. Then another breath comes and it goes. This is clearly witnessed again and again. To establish ourselves in the meditation on impermanence, through applied mindfulness and reflection, develops confidence and understanding to deal with unexpected and unwelcome changes.

We have the potential to be calm and clear about impermanence even as Nature squeezes the last breath out of our body to mark our closure with existence.

INQUIRY

1. *What is the relationship between impermanence and letting go?*

2. *Meditation on death can contribute to wisdom in life. Why?*

3. *Who or what do you take for granted?*

4. *At times, we all believe impermanence is good, not good, both, or neither. What consolidates your view and any associated pleasure or pain that arises?*

5. *What is the relationship between impermanence and inner security?*

6. *If impermanence is the conventional reality, what is the ultimate truth of things?*

7. *What is behind the curtain of change?*

Suffering

As countless Western tourists travel to Buddhist countries in Asia, it is not unusual for them to express appreciation for the happy and polite manner of the people they meet. Westerners respond enthusiastically to the warmth and kindness of the Tibetans. Thailand is known as the 'Land of Smiles'. The Burmese are hospitable. No doubt the people of these countries would attribute their day-to-day happiness to the Buddhist tradition. They have inspired numerous visitors to take a deeper interest in the teachings.

As the years pass by, we begin to see that Thai, Tibetan and other Buddhist cultures are similar to our own. A fourteen-day holiday tells us little. It never reveals the whole picture and can lead to a generalised view. Every culture, every society has its problems, its unexamined areas. Cultural attitudes get ignored. A nation can turn upon itself, as the example of Cambodia tragically shows. The greatest safeguard against suffering is not religion, but wisdom. We need to be wise about the ways of the mind, and the ways of the world. Suffering is pervasive. It never respects religious beliefs, political structures, or the nation state.

When we reflect along these lines, it can appear selfish to meditate on coming out of personal suffering. It can sound like a strategy of the ego, pursuing even more self-interest. But if we don't attend to our inner life, we will never know the way out of the problems of existence. Personal circumstances and roles can include an immense range of suffering. To examine suffering means facing every factor that contributes to it.

It is not unusual to make the excuse that we have no time to attend to the mind. Driven onwards, we go from one thing to another. Various impulses push us along. We may find ourselves like a fly stuck in the web of things, with little real movement. There are countless faces of suffering in life. Suffering connects itself with what arises, with what stays, and with what passes away. If we meditate on the impermanence of things, we can get insight into how we have sown seeds of suffering in the past. In time, seeds grow until they ripen in the present without our realising that this has been taking place. Because of this, we experience results that are undesirable and disagreeable. If we blame ourselves or others it only inflames the situation. It cannot produce resolution.

To give us more insight into resolving suffering, the Buddha taught that there are four ways of undertaking things:

1. There is a way of undertaking things that is satisfactory now and will ripen in the future as satisfactory. For example, we take pleasant medicine now and we get well.

2. There is way of undertaking things that is unsatisfactory now and will ripen in the future as satisfactory. We take bitter medicine now and we get well.

3. There is a way of undertaking things that is satisfactory now and will ripen in the future as unsatisfactory. We take pleasant medicine now and we don't get well.

4. There is a way of undertaking things that is unsatisfactory now and will ripen in the future in an unsatisfactory way. We take bitter medicine now and we don't get well.

We sometimes regard the Dharma as a pleasant or bitter medicine to cure the problems of daily life. The suffering of the inner life gives shape to our view of the world. When our story is painful, it reveals itself like an ugly train of events. Our dissatisfaction can make us question the meaning and purpose of existence. In our more optimistic moments, we like to see a purpose behind everything. In our more pessimistic moments, we can't see a purpose behind anything. Our feelings and thoughts in any given moment convince us one way or the other.

Suffering – physical, mental, emotional and spiritual – makes it hard to be in this world. We might sometimes catch ourselves looking around in a public place and thinking that nearly everybody will be dead within a hundred years. The dramas and joys of life will cease when consciousness ceases to function. Death belongs to all of us as much as anything else. There is nothing depressing about this thought; it is a simple observation of a condition that binds us.

There is much speculation about future rebirths and other planes of existence, but the rebirth of the suffering ego in the here and now matters more than this. The idea of total extinction of our existence at death seems no more reasonable than the idea of some form of continuity. The awareness of death can energise or depress the awareness of life. It can give it urgency and wonder, or it can reduce our life to a dream-world and produce doubts about the point of doing anything. Meditation on death can have a sobering effect on numerous activities. It can temper greed, lust, anger and confusion. It can make us stay very present in this moment of life.

We never know how close we are to death. It can be much closer than we think. He was a good man; cheerful, easy-going and much loved by family and friends. In his early 40s, he was married with two children. There had been a nagging pain in his liver that he kept to himself. He convinced himself there was nothing to worry about. After all, he didn't smoke or drink and took care with his weight and diet. Finally, the pain got too severe. Reluctantly he visited his doctor at the local surgery in the rural district where he lived.

The doctor ordered a blood test. Within 24 hours, the doctor called the patient to his clinic. Standing beside the doctor was a counsellor. The doctor said: 'I have some terrible news. You have cancer of the liver. Is it too far gone.' The blood dropped out of the man's face. He went ashen white. He asked the doctor: 'How long do I have?' The doctor said: 'About seven days.' The patient died about ten days later.

It seems absurd to get caught up in the materialism of the age. If we truly attend to life rather than self, we will find the dignity of consciousness. We become more attentive to the dewdrop on early morning plants, the bird on the wing, a little child playing, and gestures that go unspoken. If we are not prepared to buy into the self-centred world, we will sense the sweetness of existence. The painful story of existence begins to fade into the background.

In these realisations there isn't fear or ambiguity. We cultivate an awareness that treats each day as it comes. The cycle of birth, sickness, ageing and death need not be our only world. Having expanded the scope of our awareness, we sense it fits into something greater. All of our activities belong to a greater understanding. We see ourselves in a larger picture.

These perceptions have an impact on our feelings and thoughts. We relate to suffering in a different way. The beliefs that thought and suffering belong to 'me' become questionable. They arise from causal conditions. They may be known or unknown, explicable or inexplicable. It does not matter much. The mutual grip of suffering and self fades, but it does not leave us indifferent. Far from it. Their dissolution releases extraordinary awareness from one day to the next. There is a natural wish to contribute to dissolving the problems of life wherever they are located. We share what we have in common. We have looked the tiger in the face and realised it has no teeth.

INQUIRY

1. *What is unsatisfactory about being driven by desire?*

2. *Why are roles and suffering easily bound up together?*

3. *Do you see yourself in the larger picture of life?*

4. *What does it mean to expand your awareness?*

5. *Have you experienced that which is Immeasurable?*

Not-self

Perhaps the most difficult concept of all to understand in the teachings of the Buddha is not-self. It is an understanding that seems removed from our everyday comprehension of the ways things are. It seems utterly incongruous to show a severe doubt in the self. We experience our self as the most obvious, immediate and present thing. It is not surprising that many people find they simply cannot comprehend the teachings of not-self.

When our immediate attention turns to our self, we would say, '*I* exist in the world. *I* was born. *I* grew up. *I* became a child. *I* grew further and became an adult. *I* am making this journey through life.

I have a personal history which influences *me* in various ways in the present as it will do in the future. At some point, in the future, *I* will die. Day by day, *I* experience that *I* am getting older. *I* have a variety of roles and *I* live in a field of changing experiences.' This description applies to every adult living in the world. We cannot imagine questioning the authority of the self and its past, present and future.

If we wanted to begin to try to understand the teaching of not-self, we could take a scientific viewpoint and view ourselves as energy, including the self, states of mind, and body. We could say we are nothing but energy. However, there is nowhere in Dharma teachings where the self of heart, mind and body is described as energy. So if it's not energy, then what do we mean when we look into not-self?

Firstly, any meaningful inquiry into the construction of self requires a meditative mode of awareness and stillness of being. In this meditative state, we can ask, 'Is mind-body self or is mind-body not-self?' At times, the experience of *I*, the experience of *my*, can appear to be very substantial, bound up with mind and body. When we are caught up in the forces of attraction and aversion, wanting and rejecting, intense liking or hating, the experience of self appears very strong. The experience of *I* and *my* becomes aroused when exposed to fear. There are other times when the experience of self is much lighter: there is an expansive sense with no substance to *I*; there is contentment; feelings are bright, spacious and happy. Yet whether the self is highly charged with fear, or light and spacious, we still have the sense and view, understandably enough, of continuity of the *I*. We forget that *I* has attached itself to a state of mind, whether happy or unhappy, and vice versa.

There are also times when the *I* is not present to consciousness. The most obvious example of this is in deep sleep. Someone could be looking at us when we sleep, pulling faces at us and quietly making our room untidy. Yet there is no self arising to get upset. In deep sleep, the *I* and *my* do not arise. This also applies to certain depths of meditation. The *I* and *my* can temporarily evaporate. Afterwards, the *I* may arise and claim ownership over these experiences. If the *I* did not arise, our experience could be regarded simply as an experience, not as *my* experience. An experience is an experience. The *I* is just an I. They do not have to collide. The experience can be witnessed as self. It can also be witnessed as not-self. The sense and notion of *I* is *dependently arising*.

Meditation supports witnessing where the *I* arises. The teachings point out that this *I* is limited to five specific areas, called the Five Aggregates – material form (primarily the body), feelings, perceptions, mental formations (including thoughts), and consciousness.

1. When I say, 'I sit here' – this is *I* arising in relation to the body.
2. When I say, 'I feel content' – this is *I* arising in relationship to feelings.
3. When I say, 'I see the contents of the room' – this is *I* arising in relationship to perception.
4. When I say, 'I am thinking about the question' – this is *I* arising in relationship to thought.
5. When I say, 'I am aware' – this is *I* arising in relationship to consciousness.

When the *I* arises in one area, such as the body, it does not arise elsewhere in that moment. When the self arises in one of the Five Aggregates, the other four Aggregates become not-self in that moment. It we give substance to that which has no inherent substance, we can easily get obsessive about aspects of the body, heart and mind. It is equally no wonder we get obsessive when we keep going on about one aspect of one of the Five Aggregates. The intensification of *I* generates the ego and perpetuates the force of desire and attachment.

We may get the idea that we have to build up our self in order to lose our self. Nothing could be further from reality. Building up *I* and *my* is a disastrous undertaking. We get the idea that if we have a low sense of self-worth, we must create more *I* and *my*. The lack of self-worth is charged with *I* and *my*. If we are under pressure, the mind will always produce doubts about our self-worth. Then the self will look to our own mind or to the mind of others for approval. That's hazardous.

Teachings on *not-I, not-self, not mine* serve the deepest interests of those with an exaggerated sense of their own importance *and* those with a very low sense of self-worth. Both types of personality end up feeding on each other. Contemplation of the Five Aggregates as not-self offers freedom from the inflated and deflated self. Naturally, the mind will protest about the teachings of not-self. We have become used to identifying with each of the Five Aggregates, positively and negatively. We think this belief keeps us in touch with reality. The teachings encourage us to question this belief, but initially we need the faith to doubt the standpoints of the self.

The teachings of not-self are not an ideological declaration of the way things are. They present a radical alternative to the assumption that all experiences of body and mind are self. If there was any intelligence in the self, we would not create unhappiness for ourselves. We would no longer feel moody, hurt, angry and anxious. What self would choose that? If there was intelligence in the self, it would abandon immediately all anguish and pain. This is all not-self. The whole process of the human being is dependently arising.

This understanding dissolves the myth that our self exists independently. Its appearance depends on circumstances. There is no permanent location for self, no place to posit its position. Meditation on not-self, insight into self-inflation, and dissolving painful beliefs in lack of self-worth will dissolve self-preoccupation. From this clarity a steady presence emerges. Realising the emptiness of *I* and *my*, experience and insight into the nature of not-self is liberating.

Wisdom of not-self even dissolves the substantial view of '*I* am born and *I* will die.' We may begin to conclude, 'Oh, it is *I* who understands this. It is *my* understanding.' Yet the understanding of things also belongs to this extraordinary field of dependent arising, not to *I* and *my*.

It would be a pity to ignore questioning the self, to ignore the opportunity to awaken. Consciousness is revealed as consciousness, contents are revealed as contents. That is the sublime sweetness in all of this. When the *I* no longer swings backwards and forwards between consciousness and its contents, the world as we know it no longer holds sway. The problem of self has gone. Without the weight of *I* and *my*, all things are at peace. This peace goes beyond all our attempts to comprehend it. It is deathless.

INQUIRY

1. *What do you do to inflate your ego?*
2. *What do you appreciate about your life that challenges lack of self-worth?*
3. *Where does the self alight?*
4. *What shows the experience of not-self?*
5. *What shows the experience of freedom from clinging to self?*

FOUR FOUNDATIONS
OF AWARENESS

The knower and the known bear no substance,
Entangled perceptions for the self.
The worldly and spiritual loses its tone
When the knower no longer pushes forward
On to the fictions of the known.
Unfixed, unformed, unmarked,
Emptiness makes all things possible.

Introduction

'Four Foundations of Awareness' is the most venerated talk given by the Buddha on meditation and daily life practice for insight and immediate liberation. The practice overcomes distress, grief and despair. It makes the mind clear. It exposes the joy of Nirvana. The Four Foundations are to see:

1. Body as body.
2. Feelings as feelings.
3. Mental states as mental states.
4. Dharma as the Dharma.

Buddhist meditation draws much of its inspiration from the Buddha's teachings on these Four Foundations. It has become the most celebrated talk of the Buddha due to the practical guidance it offers. The talk has inspired more than a hundred generations of men and women to meditate and apply awareness to the immediacy of their existence.

The Buddha says we practise meditation and mindfulness so that we 'abide independently and do not cling to anything in the

140

world.' He encourages paying attention to life and death. For example, upon seeing a corpse one should remind oneself 'this body is of the same nature. It will become like that corpse. It is not exempt from that fate.' The Buddha suggests seeing 'there is body just to the extent necessary for knowing and awareness.' He does not demand mindfulness in every moment.

We see body as body *to the extent necessary* so that we abide free from clinging. He takes the same approach with the other three Foundations of Awareness and, essentially, points out:

When we are aware of arising, we do not cling to a nihilistic view of things.

When we are aware of passing, we do not cling to a lasting view of things.

When we are aware of arising and passing, moment to moment, we see into the here and now.

The Buddha says we do not have to engage in such insight meditations for seven years – we can realise total liberation within a week. After the Buddha spoke, the practitioners rejoiced and delighted in what he said.

Body

The life of the body ranks first in our consideration of all the material forms we are in contact with. In many ways it's an awesome thing to have been born into this world. If our life does not end early, we move through birth, childhood, youth, adulthood, old age and death. We can enjoy our body. When we feel energetic, fit and vital, we experience the pleasures of the body. We experience it through a good meal, a work-out, and the sweet pleasures of making love. We enjoy the body in the calmness of meditation. We enjoy seeing a beautiful person. We do not need to be a biologist to appreciate and delight in the wonder and miracle of physical existence.

Do we stop and take time to contemplate the body sitting, walking, standing and reclining? Are we mindful of the daily cycle of eating, drinking, urinating and defecating? Are we mindful when we bend, stretch, turn our head in one direction or the other? Get dressed, undressed? Are we appreciative of the body's recuperative powers, versatility and limits?

There are also the hard truths of bodily life. We might call them the less-than-pleasant features of the body. The Buddha uses the term *asubha*. *Subha* means 'beautiful'. *Asubha* means 'not beautiful'. (Sometimes Buddhist scholars have translated *asubha* as 'ugliness'.) The Buddha lists some of these *asubha* features, including urine, excrement, pus, phlegm, and so forth. For most of us, there is a natural reluctance to handle such features of bodily life.

What ways can we explore a balance between attraction towards the beautiful and aversion towards the not-beautiful? One way is to meditate on the the body as these four elements:

1. Earth – revealed as hardness, such as bones.
2. Air – revealed as movement, such as inhaling and exhaling.
3. Fire – revealed as heat, such as bodily temperature.
4. Water – revealed as cohesion, such as blood that keeps the life-force together.

Instead of saying frequently and glibly, 'Oh I'm feeling heavy/hot/sweating,' we simply observe the body in its simple elemental form so that, 'there is a feeling of heaviness' might be a more apt description. This is not a withdrawal from the body. Far from it. It is an intimacy with bodily life so that we learn to see and acknowledge it as it is.

PRACTICE

1. *Look in the mirror, preferably one that shows as much of your naked body as possible.*

2. *Turn your attention to various parts of the body, starting with the top of the head, and move your attention from one area to another.*

3. *Be aware of any conditioned reaction to any parts of the body. Observe that conditioned reaction as simply that.*

4. *Turn your attention to the whole body. Be steadfastly free from judgemental attitudes.*

It doesn't require a great deal of common sense to know that the body changes year in and year out. As we get older we are often desperately keen to look younger. Fear of growing old, attachment to the past, and denial influence our perception. We resist putting the numbers together that state our age. It's easy to forget the fact that youth, health and beauty give rise to old age, diminishing health, and usually a lack of sensual attractiveness.

At nearly fifty, Angela had four grown-up children. In the local market, she spotted a handsome young man of about twenty-two. She felt the power of attraction towards him and gave him a knowing smile. He looked at her in a startled fashion. She said afterwards that for a moment she had completely forgotten her age. She had become a twenty-year-old again, but then it was back to reality – a greying mother. 'Who is going to look at me? I'm past it,' she said. We can long for what was, be disappointed with what is, and worry about what will be. But the physical features of growing old don't have to end up as nostalgia for past beauty.

Awareness and attitude act as lord over the body. One can have the direct experience of the body in its simple form of elements, sensations, colours, movements and senses. Learning to be clear and comfortable with the range of perceptions is a practice and skill. Without such a practice we may face despair. We can use the body to puff ourselves up or put ourselves down, or we can simply see *body as body*.

FOUR POSTURES

Sitting Meditation:
Sit cross-legged, using a meditation stool or chair without back support (unless necessary). Gently roll your hips forward so that your stomach and your trunk of the body expand. Sit with your back straight, hips gently rolled forward, chin slightly tucked in, eyes closed, with a feeling of expansion in the chest and diaphragm area. Avoid the use of will-power to hold your posture. Let the whole body settle into the posture with alert presence. Bring your full awareness of the immediacy of things towards insight and realisation.

Walking Meditation:
Meditative walking consists of slow, short steps; the heel of one

foot hardly goes in front of the toes of the other. Be mindful of each foot touching the ground. Your neck and head should be straight, with shoulders relaxed. Use your eyes purely for seeing ahead and balance. Rest one hand on the other at the abdomen. Take between five and fifteen metres to walk mindfully up and down grounded in moment-to-moment awareness. Be respectful of each step on the earth. This is to empty the indulging mind, explore focused movement and awaken understanding.

Standing Meditation
Stand with your toes and heels close together, and your hands together on your abdomen. Your eyes can be closed or open. Experience the presence of the whole body from the soles of your feet to the top of your head. Experience stillness of posture, the vibration of life, and a liberating sense of being.

Reclining Meditation:
Lie flat on your back with your heels together, or bend your knees so your heels are drawn close to your buttocks. Your head should rest on a firm pillow, or two or three books. Rest your arms at the side of your body, palms facing upwards. Close your eyes. Be fully present to intimacy with immediate nature, free from clinging to *I* and *my*.

Eating Meditation
Preferably (for the sake of animals, birds and fish), eat vegetarian or vegan food. First reflect on the world-wide interdependency that makes a meal possible. Maintain silence and an alert posture throughout the meal. Eat consciously and without hurry, being mindful of tasting, chewing and swallowing the food. Conclude by reflecting on your appreciation for the meal.

It is hardly surprising that we identify to such a degree with the body. On multiple occasions through the course of a single day the *I* enters into association with it. To meditate on the body as body liberates consciousness from the burden of clinging to body. *Meditate on the body as body, as elements, as organic life, as an expression of nature; not as* I, me *or* mine. To realise this unmistakably clearly allows body to be body without the weight of self.

There are those who advocate an ageless body. Who are they kidding? In the Dharma there is no such reality in all the realms of sentient life. Body ages. When I was a wandering monk in India, I met a very old yogi living in a bamboo hut by the Ganges. He was 128 years old. I had no problem believing him. He honestly didn't look a day younger. Liberation is ageless, timeless and indestructible.

INQUIRY

1. *Do you calmly accept and understand all features of your body?*

2. *What is your relationship to diet, exercise and posture?*

3. *Are you willing to engage in the practice of seeing body as body?*

4. *Do you ever visit a cemetery for some quiet reflection on life and death?*

5. *What takes priority? Enlightenment or making endless efforts to appear young? (The former will bring great joy, the latter is a forlorn endeavour.)*

Feelings

To know ourselves is a responsibility. Knowing ourselves includes the ability to track what we think and feel about anything that matters to us. When we pay attention, we notice the initial contact that we make with a person or object. That object may be a memory, thought about the future or the raw sense data coming through our senses. From this contact, a feeling arises. This feeling may be pleasant. It may be unpleasant. It may be neither pleasant nor unpleasant. We act under the influence of this feeling whether we know it or not.

From this feeling arises a perception. What happens after this tells us what kind of person we are. Attraction towards the object may arise from pleasant feelings. Aversion may arise from unpleasant feelings. Indifference may arise from feelings neither pleasant or unpleasant. We can find ourselves pulled magnetically towards the object that pleasant feelings have latched on to. Sometimes we are helpless in the force of that desire. There is then no capacity to stop, to stand steady amidst that magnetic impulse. From the unpleasant feeling, there may arise dislike, rejection and avoidance. We want to see the extinction of the unpleasant feeling, so we put it down, undermine it, get rid of it.

With the feeling neither pleasant nor unpleasant, we may get stuck in a neutral state of mind lacking in any obvious feeling. Things don't feel particularly pleasant or unpleasant. We feel a certain indifference or aloofness in our mind to our emotional life. We may delude ourselves into thinking that we are objective when we minimise feelings. But since we build up our relationship to the world upon the pleasant, unpleasant and the feeling in-between, we identify with the way we feel. It influences what we say and what we do and makes it very difficult to be objective.

We keep associating with an unpleasant feeling purely in problematic terms. This is all too human. It becomes hard to imagine any other way of looking at the situation. We cannot see the truth behind the belief that we have built up over time. Unless we develop a strong foundation of equanimity, unless we find the resolve to examine the situation, we too may hit a wall.

We grasp on to and identify ourselves with that object of interest from past, present or future. Thus the *I* builds up its world from contact and interpretation of the three kinds of feelings. This process of contact, feelings, desire and identification sets up a momentum. The self becomes helplessly intertwined in this interpretation of psychological events. We often give exaggerated authority to the standpoint emerging from reactivity. We say to ourselves and others: 'It must be true, because I feel it.' Or we say the opposite: 'It must be true because I am not letting my feelings get in the way.' We often forget that our feelings and thoughts can change dramatically. We also notice that our thoughts act as a fuel for our feelings and perceptions – like putting paper and wood on the fire.

We remember a situation from the past, either pleasant or unpleasant, and then begin to think about it. The thinking fuels the feeling. We can feel thrilled and excited, based on the pleasant feeling. We can also feel terribly low. For that fuelling to take place requires the interaction of thoughts and feelings. This affects our body experiences and sensations. Yet there are also feelings and thoughts that are too subtle for body sensations. It is as though the body sensations are our outer clothes, the gross body. Sometimes we only experience the subtle body, namely the mind, with its feelings, thoughts, perceptions and inner movement.

We can bring our feelings to awareness and explore handing the spectrum of them wisely and skilfully. If we don't, we are then subjected to a range of problems. The first is the suffering born of selfishness, based on clinging to pleasant feelings. We unwisely assume that identifying with a certain feeling is beneficial for the self. There is suffering born of clinging to an unpleasant feeling that can lead to deep unhappiness. There is suffering born of clinging to the feeling neither pleasant nor unpleasant. This stops us from expressing our feelings. It neutralises the activity of the heart and makes us seem rather cold.

We can easily go about our day in a mechanical way, out of touch with our feelings. There is a failure to notice the signals before we crash. Under the weight of our feelings and thoughts, we build up pressure and stress through ignoring them. Spellbound by various desires and views, we forget the underlying support for them from the three types of feelings.

Some people will say: 'There is nothing much going on in my life. Nothing grips me.' It is hardly surprising that the drugs and alcohol industry are booming. They offer an opportunity to experience different feelings, to have an altered state of consciousness. People want to feel differently from how they are feeling. It we go deeply into ourselves, experience deep intimacy with the here and now, we get a tremendous amount of nourishment through all our senses. Not only that, we can experience significant altered states of consciousness that are genuinely heart-opening. There are meditation tools and resources available to help us contact these experiences.

The pursuit of pleasure and suppression of pain are transformed through a consciousness that is open and expansive. The world of the pleasant, the unpleasant, and feelings neither pleasant nor unpleasant, has its place, but in a remarkably different way from what the conventional mind thinks. To know this takes a fundamentally altered state of consciousness, not the temporary kind that arises through brief stimulation.

PRACTICE

1. *Give particular attention to one of the three types of feelings (pleasant, unpleasant or neither) for a day.*

2. *Notice what the mind does with the particular feeling.*

3. *Practise cultivating a beneficial response and letting go of an unwise one.*

4. *Develop the practice to include all three types of feelings regularly.*

5. *What is truly sublime?*

Mental States

Mental states can be satisfying or unsatisfying. We find we experience movement between these two dualities. Due to lack of inner understanding, we keep trying to produce pleasant states of mind, while resisting unpleasant ones, through identification with standpoints. It can become all too easy to cling to one side of the duality or the other. The Buddha has given a list of some of the dualities of the mind. They include:

1. Mind blindly in pursuit of things. Mind that isn't.
2. Mind caught up in negativities, resentment and hostility. Mind that isn't.
3. Mind in confusion. Mind that isn't.
4. Mind that is contracted and suppressed. Mind that isn't.
5. Mind that is distracted. Mind that isn't.
6. Mind in *samadhi*. Mind that isn't.
7. Mind that is high. Mind that isn't.
8. Mind that is free. Mind that isn't.

Where the mental state is problematic, we develop the capacity to observe it. We see feelings, thoughts and perceptions forming together to produce various states of mind. We observe that thoughts have an impact on the emotions, and emotions have an impact on thoughts. An intense mind-state or experience often leaves a residue of impression. So even though the drama of it fades away, we carry the memory. The condition of the memory may influence the future activities of our body, speech and mind in unhealthy ways. It may cause the previous situation to flare up again. The more we hold on to the memory, the more we live under the influence of the past.

In the midst of a painful mind-state, we tend to look for a cause. Questioning often begins with 'why?' The way the mind responds to this question may be helpful or it may be a problem. Reflection can help us to understand, or fuel the mind-state. If we keep repeating the thoughts, trying to find a resolution, we make the problem worse. What is our motive for asking why? Insight into the problem dissolves the difficult state of mind, it doesn't fuel it. With insight, we genuinely learn something from the experience. It shows that we have understood our inner process. Some questioning just leads us around in circles.

Without insight into the unpleasant mental state, we are prone to repeating history. We'll make the same mistakes again and again, even when we swear black-and-blue that we won't. With practice we can see a state of mind as just a state of mind. There is less interest in fuelling it. There is greater interest in understanding it. We remain vigilant about its arising, staying and dissolution. We recognise that it is dependently arising and dependently passing. Letting go, non-attachment, acceptance, witnessing change, and insight matter. Denial, justifying, or condemning mental states are no substitute.

PRACTICE

1. *Be mindful and conscious of the here and now.*

2. *Be aware of states of mind. Be aware of the desire for the opposite when suffering arises in the mind.*

3. *Notice times of pure observation of the state of mind and times of being lost in it.*

4. *Regard any state of mind as an opportunity for 'self' learning and insight into inner life.*

5. *Witness a thought, opinion or judgement as just that. Know the difference between thoughts supported with wisdom and unwholesome thoughts.*

6. *See the mind as belonging to a process. Observe honestly the presence of the motivation behind your actions.*

7. *Be aware that an experience forms through conditions, not through choice.*

8. *Be aware of the interdependence of events, feelings, perceptions and consciousness forming the state of mind.*

9. *Learn to explore the depths of meditation and religious experiences. See such experiences as the opportunity for insight and realisation.*

10. *By not holding on to any experience, the heart-mind does not become the centre of existence. Realise liberation and the free mind.*

The readiness to attend to the arising and passing of mental states matters a great deal. We may become aware of the moment that an unpleasant state of mind arose. We may also become aware of our relationship to it. Is there aversion towards it or clinging to it? We need awareness to the extent necessary to free ourselves from living out painful mind-states and their consequences to ourselves and others. When we truly see the impermanence and the dependent arising of our mind-states we stop clinging to a standpoint. Clear seeing or sudden insight shakes the mind-state so that it loses its grip over consciousness.

Nina, a young lawyer, worked for a high-powered law firm. One evening, the executives invited her to join them for an expensive evening meal. Much of the communication focused around striving, success, and regularly sneering at competitors. Nina would have liked to have talked about other things more meaningful to her. When it came to ordering the meal, she ordered vegetarian. This produced some cynical comments. One of the lawyers ordered *pâté de foie gras* (goose liver). Nina knew that the geese are force-fed in order to swell up their livers before they are killed. She turned to one lawyer and asked him if he realised the fate of these birds. He replied, 'I couldn't give a damn what they do to these birds, as long as the food tastes good.' The senior lawyers perceived her as 'not one of them'. They described her as idealistic and not committed enough to the company. Her values affected her opportunity for promotion.

We may need to have an attitude of defiance when we do not subscribe to the forces of selfishness and insensitivity. It takes an act of courage to speak our mind. We need to say *no* when what we see is unjust or discriminatory. We need to dig deep into ourselves to keep faith with integrity. We should not deceive ourselves into imagining that there won't be any personal cost. It may produce more unpleasant mental states for ourselves and others, but if we go near the fire we must take the heat.

We have the opportunity to experience a remarkable freedom of mind that isn't living in the shadows of our past nor conforming to the demands of others in the present. In this freedom there is an awakening that matters more than all the success imaginable.

We would be hard-pressed to think of a situation in our life where there was suffering without clinging. The fruit of this practice allows a natural non-clinging response to circumstances of past, present and future. If we do not hold on to things that are subject to time and change, we will free ourselves from a great number of difficulties. Through such practices we find clarity of mind, emotional well-being, and the true riches of life unavailable in wealth, tradition or conventional forms of success.

If we don't understand the way things are, that there is no self in all of this – this does not belong to the self and this is not what the self is – our mind-states will be problematic. When we look upon things with clear wisdom, joy flows easily and effortlessly out of a wise abiding with the presence of life. This joy knows no opposite.

Through wisdom, we:

Engage in the practice of not clinging to objects.

Engage in the practice of not clinging to people.

Engage in the practice of not clinging to states of mind.

Engage in the practice of not clinging to the condition of the body.

Engage in the practice of not clinging to this world.

Engage in the practice of not clinging to standpoints.

Engage in the practice of staying steady with wisdom.

The Dharma

When we come to the last of the Four Foundations of Awareness, we see an immediate opening-out of the field of interest. With the first three we brought awareness to body, feelings and mental states. In the fourth Foundation, we explore the Dharma. Dharma means here firstly the teachings concerned with enlightenment, and secondly awareness of here and now. As a Foundation of Awareness, the expression of Dharma includes looking at our relationship to the Four Noble Truths, the Noble Eightfold Path, the Five Hindrances, the sense doors and sense objects. Is there a depth of awareness and wisdom in each of these areas? The Dharma as our Foundation points to enlightenment.

This fourth Foundation of Awareness reminds us to bring an expansive interest to the here and now. We can make ourselves receptive to everything arising and passing in the present. This includes sights, sounds, thoughts, and so on. We keep our body impeccably still and remain utterly present, which is a wonderful way of experiencing clarity. There is no wish nor intention of the mind to seize or grasp on to anything. Sense data barely touch our sense doors. There is no desire to make something of the silence nor to neglect it.

The *I* and *my* lose their significance. Fantasies, projections and ideas drop away. There is a luminous transparency in this experience. We see the wisdom of not grasping after anything. This exposure to a choiceless awareness grounds us in a remarkable way. This kind of meditation serves as an open doorway to an undivided life. Such awareness brings us closer to the truth of things. We experience in this immediacy the liberating Dharma of life.

Though we may endeavour to extend the field of *mine* to include more, it will always be a tiny drop in the ocean. Not surprisingly, it brings little lasting satisfaction. We can never get enough. The more we have, the more we want. If we live in the world of *mine* and *not mine*, we live in a state of fragmentation. Seeing this, the endless pursuit of self-gratification becomes empty. We discover the sense of the unshakeable nature of things that holds everything easily and effortlessly.

Dharma is not God. When we create God, we also create prayers and forms of worship. Prayers can uplift the spirit or reinforce the small, fearful self wanting something more. The Dharma of Awareness explores the fearful self. Instead of prayer there is meditation on life. There is no self-hypnosis, mind-control techniques, mantras or other religious attributes. There is the direct connection with the immediacy of things. This leaves the potential for us to realise something timeless. In the clear exposure to the here and now, we are knocking on the door to awakening. The capacity to see things clearly comes through different resources:

1. Reflection.
2. Meditation.
3. Inquiry.
4. Listening to teachings.
5. Speaking.
6. Reading.
7. Contact with nature.

1. **Reflection** brings attention to experiences and the teachings. There is a difference between thinking about and reflection. Thinking about doesn't make much difference to the situation. We can think and think, tie ourselves up in a knot of thinking, and not find any resolution. Reflection has an authority to it. We can sense that it is making a difference; we can feel we are moving towards clarity.

2. **Meditation.** The shift from thinking to reflection requires a level of calmness. Meditation practice develops calmness. It can be worthwhile to set time aside to reflect on a situation. The questions that we ask matter. Unwise, prejudiced reflection leads nowhere. If we pull a cow by the horns, it won't produce milk. Meditation and reflection often go hand-in-hand. Meditation without reflection may contribute to calmness but not necessarily to the power of wisdom. Reflecting without meditation may only develop an intellectual understanding.

3. **Inquiry.** There is self-inquiry through reflection, and inquiry with others. This is the capacity of two or more people to meet together to look into issues that matter to them all, asking questions and being asked questions. Inquiry can shake us up. It can touch all manner of deep places within. It gets us to reflect in different ways on issues of importance. Inquiry contributes to right understanding.

4. **Listening to teachings** provides insight and inspiration.

One point in a talk can touch the deepest place within. It can open up whole new avenues. We experience the common sense and wisdom of what we hear. In listening we need to use our discernment. Unlike religious belief systems, Dharma teachings require the listener to apply discernment to see what works, what proves beneficial, and what enlightens consciousness. It is extremely unlikely that we will agree with everything we hear.

Teachings can be provocative, challenging some of our deeply cherished beliefs. Teachers are human as well and may come out with remarks that are unskilful, not commensurate with the Dharma. Teachers need feedback so they also have an opportunity for reflection and insight. Listening to teachings of liberation stands as one of the most powerful resources for an enlightened life.

5. **Speaking** about the Dharma of life can also be extraordinarily insightful. We do not need a particular role or level of authority for this. Insights can flower through communication and sharing our experience. Speaking insightfully is not something for the self to grasp hold of in order to build up pride. Wisdom emerges out of the selfless nature of things, not from the ego of *I* and *my*.

6. **Reading** for insight and wisdom contributes to finding wisdom. The attitude in such reading must be different from conventional reading. Conventional reading arises to pass the time, to acquire information, for pleasure or analysis. Reading for insight and wisdom is neither for pleasure nor intellectual satisfaction. Dharma reading is mindful, conscious and receptive. We adopt a respectful posture.

During the course of reading there may be a phrase, sentence or theme that our heart responds to. We let our heart absorb what touches us. Perhaps we walk meditatively up and down reflecting on our response. The Dharma journey goes from head to heart. We may go back over that passage again later. If we really allow ourselves to read in an unhurried, respectful fashion, we can allow profound literature to awaken our lives. Monks and nuns often go into solitude armed with just a few collections of verses

7. **Contact with nature.** We probably all pay lip-service to the value of spending time in nature. To walk in the hills, to spend time on a deserted beach, to sit at the foot of a tree in the forest, establishes a natural communion with nature. The meetings of the

natural elements of earth, air, sun, water and space spark an inner response. We can forget our everyday public self to feel a deep oneness with life.

We can explode the myth that enlightenment belongs to saints and sages who live an unconventional life. Liberation is available to us all, here and now. We have so much potential, so much to discover. No discovery can match the realisation of that which is both causeless and deathless.

INQUIRY

1. *What can you discover?*
2. *What is an adventure in consciousness?*
3. *What would open out your life?*
4. *What do thoughts and leaves have in common?*
5. *What is your true nature?*

FIVE PRECEPTS

We have hurt, harmed and fought
Each other, these troubles beat,
Until clarity pervades our heated cells,
We live upon the cry of pain and grief.

Introduction

Five Precepts serve as the moral basis of the teaching. They are:

1. To refrain from killing.
2. To refrain from stealing.
3. To refrain from sexual harm.
4. To refrain from lying.
5. To refrain from abuse of intoxicants.

Three aspects of the Noble Eightfold Path embrace morality: right speech, right action and right livelihood. The Five Precepts make wisdom and conduct shine. A common element for the mind with each of them is restraint. Through restraint we ward off unhealthy tendencies that cause suffering for others, ourselves, or both.

Evil in the world is associated directly with the refusal to show respect to the Five Precepts. It is not unusual that disregard for any one of them leads to abuse of the remaining four.

There is a common view that abstaining and restraint are negative attitudes. The positive outcome of respecting the Five Precepts is:

1. To protect life.
2. To offer security to people's goods and money.
3. To give safety and health to adults and children.
4. To speak what is true and useful.
5. To keep us mindful and healthy.

Not Killing

As a member of the international board of the Buddhist Peace Fellowship, I wrote a peace treaty which I offer to all those who remain determined to find ways to resolve conflicts without resorting to force. I hand it out on retreats, workshops and campaigns as well as on the Internet! I call it the People's Peace Treaty:

I vow to observe and respect the following:

1. I vow to dissociate myself completely from any destruction of life, including all acts of war, acts of terror and executions. I will not support any declarations of war initiated by my country or any other that I support.

2. I vow not to attack or abuse other groups of people (nations, majorities, minorities or individuals).

3. I vow to give support to organisations and groups working for peace, justice, political, economic and environmental rights.

4. I vow to work to end suffering perpetuated through violence, fear, corruption, phobias or greed.

5. I will endeavour to persuade the military, arms manufacturers and arms dealers to lay down their weapons and kill the hate inside themselves.

6. I vow to see people rather than the labels attached to people, and to be aware of our common humanity.

7. I vow to work to end anger, aggression or fear within myself, as an expression of duty to humanity.

Politicians and the media easily manipulate the public emotion of loyalty. We feel that if we criticise our government for supporting certain wars, armed conflicts and arms sales we are betraying our country. We are often naive when we believe that a military agenda is for the common good. Weapons and killing belong to a world of huge egos. One nineteen-year-old US soldier who was shot in the chest in a skirmish in Vietnam told me, 'Soldiers who are young, poor and powerless follow the orders of the old, rich and powerful to go and kill other men who are young, poor and powerless. Our enemies were young guys much like ourselves. We had more in common with them than with our leaders.' Innocent citizens, from babies in arms to elderly people, suffer in regional conflicts. They are the victims of the egos of people with power.

We identify with the views of our leaders, imagining that they are essentially right or only a little misguided. We believe that the other nation is a threat and that its people are somehow inferior. We fail to see that acts of state terrorism, such as bombing from the air, are as indiscriminate as a terrorist organisation's bombs on the ground. Unless we free ourselves from the emotion of loyalty, we can never look at the total situation – namely what people do to each other. Loyalty is no substitute for the wisdom of protest against the killing machines and the obscene reprisals of governments and organisations.

A woman telephoned me while I was giving teachings in the USA. She asked if she could have a one-to-one meeting. I said that I could only spare a few minutes as my days were already full. She said it was urgent, and offered to drive me across the city to my next workshop so that we could talk in the car. I agreed.

Ten years previously she had visited a country in Central America. There she had witnessed for herself the violence and aggression of the US-backed military regime. In the villages the soldiers mutilated the men, raped the women and hacked children to death. She joined the militant left. She fought in skirmishes, imported weapons and acted as a gun-runner. 'There was no other choice,' she told me. 'I couldn't turn my back on these people. I had many friends who died, disappeared or were tortured by the regime. The practice of *ahimsa* [non-violence] means nothing in that country. I want to go on believing it was right to fight the government, the military and secret police. I am trying to resolve the conflicts inside myself. Some people agree with me. Some people disagree with me.'

In such a situation, there is no point in preaching about the morality of protecting life. There is no point in stating that killing begets killing, violence begets violence. It sounds like the rhetoric of the pacifist. Revenge, fear and mistrust dominate the psyche of the militant. When we take up sides we take up arms. It is so easy to pronounce on such matters when it is not our family and friends who are being hacked to death. It is easy to justify killing soldiers. After all, they are not our sons.

As the woman drove me across the city, I continued to ask one question after another. She was honest and frank. We got stuck in traffic on a bridge and she was pleased. It gave her more time to talk. My questions seemed to heighten her conflict. She needed to draw out of herself every *for* and *against* view around armed conflict. Her inner condition and her outer conflict had much in common. She was at war with herself. I arrived late to give my talk. She thanked me for my time and I never saw her again. The mind is a strange thing. It can vociferously condemn others for causing suffering and justify itself for the same behaviour. To her credit, she had doubts.

We need to collectively rethink the way we relate to each other. We need moral leadership not just political leadership. We need an end to the international arms trade. We need legislation to ban firearms. Despite the endless technical difficulties, we would at least show that we are not fudging our revulsion for the ownership and use of weapons. The production of weapons is obscene, whether nuclear or conventional, anti-personnel mines or the gun.

A soldier told an interviewer that he threw up the first time he shot and killed somebody. He said he felt sick to the bottom of his guts. He stayed awake all night, full of remorse. He thought of the dead soldier's young wife and child (he found their photograph in the dead man's wallet). He thought of his parents, and the terrible weeping and sorrow at the funeral. He hated himself. His fellow soldiers in his platoon told him he would get over it. A few days later the soldier killed another of the enemy. Again, he felt intensely upset, but not as much as the first time. By the time he had killed his eighth enemy soldier, he slept well at night. Soon he was telling other young soldiers that they would get over it. The mind can get used to anything, even to killing.

Soldiers, freedom fighters, political activists and their superiors believe that they are fighting on the right side. They believe what their politicians and generals have told them. Loyalty and unquestioning obedience enable killing to take place. It is questionable whether it takes courage to follow orders to kill or whether it reveals an unthinking mind. It certainly takes moral determination to resist orders to kill.

Years ago, I used to attend a weekly meeting with a group of men serving life sentences. There was no agenda. We talked about whatever seemed appropriate. Most of the prisoners were murderers. One evening we got on to the issue of capital punishment. The majority of the lifers said they wanted to see the re-introduction of hanging in the penal system. 'That'll stop them,' they said. 'It's the only way to deal with these people. A life for a life.' I then asked the obvious question: 'So, you all feel that you should have been hanged for killing somebody?' 'Oh no, not in my case.' They then gave a list of reasons. 'Spur of the moment.' 'Manslaughter.' 'I didn't mean to hurt him.' 'The gun went off by accident.' 'The judge misled the jury.'

The resolution of conflict comes through direct, constructive engagement. We need men and women of integrity with training in the resolution of conflict. They must be free from the vested interests of their governments. We need fearless and determined men and women who command respect. For the most part, politicians and diplomats are out of their depth in such matters. Resolution of conflict comes through unambiguous respect for life, not through politicians holding a gun to the heads of men, women and children, or diplomats mouthing the words of their superiors. We need wise men and women who can let go of clinging to painful history and penetrate deep into the present. Hatred ceases through the wisdom of non-hatred, not through continuity of the past.

INQUIRY

1. *What is your response to the use of weapons by the nation state or terrorist organisation?*

2. *Have you ever had the desire to kill somebody? What built up such a desire?*

3. *Some claim life is sacred. Others say life is easily dispensable. What is your response?*

4. *Would you sanction your government to kill men, women and children on your behalf?*

5. *Teachings point to realising the Deathless. What is the relationship of this realisation to the first precept?*

Not Stealing

I once took the infamous bus that runs to and from the Vatican in central Rome. It is regarded as a vehicle for thieves. Crowded with tourists and citizens of the city, the bus made its way through the streets. Suddenly all hell broke loose and a Korean family began yelling and shouting. The father grabbed a young Italian boy who had taken his wallet. The Italian protested his innocence, but one of the Korean children saw him pass the wallet over to an accomplice, who then passed it on to another. The mother was crying, another child repeatedly hit the thief on the chest. The driver stopped the bus, used the central locking system, and waited for the police. The furore continued, with more and more passengers becoming involved in a yelling match. The behaviour of a minority had affected the innocent majority.

I met Tony when he was serving a six-year sentence for bank robbery. He had moved in a circle of thieves and robbers. In the next cell was Jim, a professional burglar. He told me that he could rob fifteen to twenty-five houses a night. He would park his van in the street of a leafy suburb and systematically break in, even taking handbags off bedside tables. Neither Tony nor Jim showed any remorse for their actions. Tony told me that he would 'never stoop so low as to rob the gas meters of old ladies.' His next job, he said, was to make a small fortune out of an insurance scam.

People who have their possessions stolen feel personally violated. Stealing, cheating, embezzlement, financial exploitation, all invade the inner life of others. Subjected to a robbery or cheated financially, the victims feel hurt, often experiencing a pain outweighing the value of what they have lost. It would be easy to put this down exclusively to personal attachment. We might conclude that suffering emerges through losing what we have. That may well be true, but it can run deeper than that. There is the violation of the recognition that we are all interconnected. Thieves, robbers and cheats undermine a natural code of respect for people and property.

We find it equally distasteful to see those who accumulate great wealth for themselves and their families, knowing it comes from exploiting others. Nothing can justify that. One injustice does not permit another. Lust for money and goods, stealing, dishonest wheeling and dealing, corrupt people's relationships with each other, near and far.

The crude mind desires to get what it wants regardless of the feelings of others. Even if Tony pulled off the insurance scam, it would not be without cost to individuals. Members of staff would endure questioning from police and bosses, with weeks of investigation and recriminations. Heavy suspicion would charge the air. What do you say to thieves and cheats? To attack them or condemn them for what they have done seems doomed to failure. Increasing their prison sentences often only lengthens the time they have to train and plan for the next job. Neither severe nor light punishment shows a track record of reducing crime. Cutting off hands, solitary confinement, banishment, long prison sentences, hard labour, short-sharp-shock treatments – make little difference.

What brings about inner change that ends the corruptions of the mind?

1. Motivation to begin the process of inner change.
2. Upholding agreements.
3. Reflection.
4. Discovery of worthwhile activities.
5. Emotional closeness to loved ones.
6. Uncovering childhood patterns.
7. Personal contact with victims.
8. The discipline of insightful meditation.
9. Working with feelings of inadequacy.
10. A transforming experience.

Grace met a young man at a party. They got on well together and after a couple of months he moved into her flat. She had inherited some money from her grandparents. The young man had some debts from a failed business venture. Gradually he coerced out of her several thousand pounds to pay off his debts. He then wanted more money to start another initiative, which she gave him. Whenever she resisted, he accused her of being tightfisted. He told her that if he made money they would both benefit.

Grace became more and more afraid of him. She told her brothers and sisters about these 'loans'. They hit the roof, accusing her of behaving irresponsibly. Her inheritance became a nightmare. The boyfriend persistently cheated her. It wasn't exactly stealing, but it was certainly grossly manipulative. He played on her vulnerabilities, fears, and lack of self-worth. He took what was reluctantly given. One day he disappeared. It took her months to get over the situation. She could not forgive him or herself.

We live in a culture constantly on the make. It seems that most people try to get away with something. Stealing can touch primal urges for revenge. It is hard to fathom the psyche of people lusting for money regardless of the effect of this on the lives of others.

When we rephrase the idea of stealing, we may have to look at ourselves more carefully. Buddhists undertake 'to train not to take that which has not been given'. Such a vow makes us aware of everything we handle. It brings a global perspective to goods rather than just a personal one. It brings ethics to money and investment. It brings sensitivity to the use of resources. The vow makes us look at times when we are avoiding payment, such as of taxes or debts.

In a Buddhist monastery, monks treat the guideline of not taking what is not given with utmost seriousness. Monks do not take the razor, book, robe or begging bowl of another monk without securing permission first. It is a discipline in letting go, in patience, in waiting for something to be available. Such a rule can be inconvenient and trying. It acknowledges the natural associations of people with items, but it is not a support for clinging and attachment. Fear of loss and separation encourage clinging and attachment. Loss or separation without understanding induces anger.

We remember to ask permission to use any items that we know belong to another. We give a high priority to respect for others. We would rather do without than take without consultation. What am

I taking from the rest of life to support my existence? What am I giving back?

Paying respect to this one precept, gross and subtle, gives support to the peace of mind of others. There is no finer service.

INQUIRY

1. *What is ethically questionable about getting away with as much as you can in matters of making a profit?*
2. *Where do you draw the line on honesty and dishonesty?*
3. *Do you have to get before you can give?*
4. *What dissolves giving and taking?*

Not Causing Sexual Harm

The current criterion for freedom of sexual activity has the proviso, 'between consenting adults' of whatever sexual orientation. This is useful since it safeguards everyone outside this category, although it cannot have a rigid definition since age and maturity vary considerably from person to person, and from culture to culture. This criterion acknowledges the rights of people who are attracted to others of the opposite gender or the same gender or either gender. Dharma teachings are concerned with causes of suffering, not gender preference.

As a society, we make general guidelines and enforce these guidelines through the law. We should not forget that 'sexual abuse' covers different categories of people who are vulnerable to suffering. These include children, minors, those under the influence of alcohol or drugs, those suffering from mental health problems or low intelligence, and anyone who actively resists engaging in sexual activity.

Those who seriously violate sexual rights are sent to prison. This offers protection to the public. Though custodial sentences keep sexually harmful people off the streets, they cannot cure the individual of his or her behaviour. That requires the presence of insightful counsellors and co-operation from the abuser. Sexual abuse has its origins in the accumulating forces in the mind. It gets unleashed on the innocence of others. Not only does this force violate others, but it degrades and humiliates them as well.

The desire to hurt and humiliate others usually springs from personal humiliation, often in childhood. Even after a healthy childhood, the lust for sex can arise, particularly in extreme conditions such as war, a sexually charged atmosphere, or under the influence of alcohol. Certain soldiers subject civilians of all ages to sexual humiliation through language, gestures and acts. Few are held accountable. Fighting, rage and forced sex often share a common bond – they destroy people's lives. Healing the emotions can take much longer than healing the body.

These forces of sexual aggression generate an outpouring of destructive feelings towards the victim. The aggressors perceive their victims as unworthy of existence. The desire to secure pleasure invites the same intensity of desire to inflict pain. Forcing sex on another is an effective way for the brutal mind to achieve both ends. It is hard to communicate the depth of the emotional trauma the victim suffers. Skilled counselling, love and understanding become vehicles for healing.

Alice told me that her husband was a commando. She noticed that he became more and more sexually aggressive towards her. She felt he was using her to overcome his fears, rage and wounded self-pride. When she spoke with a friend, an army psychologist, he said wives and girlfriends of men in the armed services regularly reported such experiences to him and he suggested that she give him an ultimatum. Either the aggression stops or she leaves. Before we can speak up, we often need the support and empathy of another to strengthen our voice.

It is also important to look at the relationship of sexual activity between consenting adults. People have the right to be discreet about their relationships involving another consenting adult. But any lies and deceit (violating the fourth Precept) often cause more suffering than the sexual act itself. Orthodox religious people still strongly condemn any sexual activity outside marriage. Some parents will throw their children out of their home for making love prior to marriage. Discretion between two people gives protection from the ugly backlash of puritans, including family members.

Two people have the right not to talk about their love-making to others. Gossip, self-righteousness, rage, religious authorities and the media can display sanctimonious attitudes about people's involvement with each other. Making love becomes a spark for hype: sex sells newspapers. Sexual events carry such a charge in our psyche that we have a strong tendency to pre-judge. We may not even know the full facts of a situation, or the people involved. Given the same situation, we might even act the same way. We need to distinguish very clearly between the principle of consenting adults on sexual matters and the sexual abuse of another person through forced sexual activity. Killing takes away the right to life of another. Stealing takes away the right to own of another. Sexual harm takes away the right of another to feel safe, secure and loved.

Like other religions, Buddhist texts condemn adultery. The concept of 'adultery' sounds like moralising. It has an accusatory tone. To embark on a sexual relationship with another adult may be inappropriate and unwise. If it is a situation between consenting adults, such an encounter must be treated in a very different light from one that inflicts suffering on an individual through forced or manipulative sex. To deliberately cause such sexual pain to somebody violates this third Precept.

Married in her early twenties, Brigitte had two children. By the time she was in her thirties any passion for her husband had long since worn off. Their sexual life was infrequent and rather ritualistic. He always initiated it. The only time he told her he loved her was after sex. She often thought, 'I have sex with my husband but we never make love.' Then she met a man at a party and they began seeing each other. After some weeks, they made love and continued their secret meetings.

'Since meeting this man, I have been much happier. I enjoy my time with my husband. I treat him as my best friend. I am much less demanding. I now feel loved and I can give more love to my family.' She risked the wrath of family and friends for this love. It is not only the churches who find such affairs intolerable; many conventional people do as well. A discreet affair can be viewed as repugnant – secrecy behind somebody's back. It is very easy to be self-righteous in such matters. Events are rarely that simple.

Perhaps two consenting adults who nourish each other through making love need understanding rather than hostile judgements, concern rather than denouncement. The so-called wronged party may have to take a share of the responsibility. Admittedly, it may only be a small share. But it may not be.

Brigitte told me that her extra-marital relationship still continued. She knew it would cause terrible pain to her husband if he found out. She knew it could result in the break-up of the family. Once trust goes it is hard to recover. Any of these considerations should send the individual alarm signals about getting involved with another person. But we are also human, all too human. Emotional nourishment may not occur within the household.

The power of love, combined with sexual attraction between consenting adults, sweeps away numerous considerations of rules, regulations, etiquette and roles. Making love, as distinct from having sex, reveals warmth and closeness. People yearn for this feeling of intimacy. Making love is one expression of it. The potential for a devastating impact upon a marriage must be considered. A secret love affair can lead to lies, deceptions, guilt and confusion. The totality of the situation must be reflected upon.

We must look at every situation with as much clarity as possible. We need to develop the capacity to see beyond the compelling attraction of one of life's most intense experiences. There is a charge around sexual matters. One extreme is suppression of sexual feelings. The other extreme is permissiveness. It is not an easy task to find the Middle Way between these two extremes. We need to listen to the wise place within. We need to learn from our mistakes so that we don't repeat history. It means listening to the clear voices of others as much as ourselves. Making love in respectful ways reveals the energetic oneness of human experience.

INQUIRY

1. *Can you talk with another about difficult sexual matters?*

2. *In what area of sexual life are you most likely to experience confusion?*

3. *Do you have views about sexuality and celibacy?*

4. *What is the relationship of sexual experience and a liberated wisdom?*

Not Lying

There is the selfish liar and there is the one lied to. Inwardly, the liar has identified himself or herself with a set of views and beliefs supported by certain intentions. The person does not want these revealed. There is a gap between their inner experience and knowledge and what they communicate. Liars are willing to say anything, make up anything, to serve their own ends. Entering into a web of deceit, the mind creates the gap between thoughts and spoken words. Liars haunt this world. Denying others the opportunity to know the truth of the matter, they say something else no matter what the cost. It's the motives behind the words that count, and the liar hates accountability.

Some lie for personal gain and cheat and manipulate the truth to their advantage. Such people care little for others. They do everything with one aim in mind – to gain advantage over others, especially those perceived as standing in the way, as competitors. They have squeezed love, compassion and natural intelligence out of their world.

The liar requires the co-operation of the one lied to. The liar depends upon the trust, acceptance and even gullibility of the other. Lies form the direction of some people's lives as much as truths. It eats away our trust when others lie to us. If it happens frequently, we will become suspicious of their intentions. It hurts when others deliberately mislead us.

There are times when we reflect circumstances honestly. We have the capacity to mirror back what we see without vested interests. There is an obvious morality in refusing to lie and deceive. There are times when we moderate the truth. The motive matters. The decision may change as circumstances change.

There are times, too, when we withhold the truth or restrain it, and times when we tell outright lies. The deliberate intention to deceive is never pleasant, even when we feel there is a sound reason. There is often some element of fear at work. In any honest examination of ourselves we see how we get caught up in a story-line. We believe or know something but say something else. Lies are a form of attack or defence. There is a pressure we are unable to resolve. We use lies as a way of escaping a difficult situation. When others question our lies, we extend the cover-up. We can then find ourselves in more hot water.

When we lie, it is a way of saying that we are not trustworthy. One of the most common reasons for lying stems from the fear of hurting others, but the uncovered lie can be far more hurtful. We don't have to explain ourselves. The basic criteria for communication is simple: speak that which is true and useful. To be sensitive and respectful to the feelings of others shows respect to ourselves. Giving false explanations, we find it harder and harder to distinguish fact from fiction. We'll swear over our mother's grave that we're telling the truth. And we're not.

Lies and self-deceptions often go hand in hand. For example, we can hide the truth from others and from ourselves. We can keep telling ourselves and others that we are very happy. We put on a face. Inside it may be a different story. It only takes one small incident to light the fire. For example, through marriage Tracy became fabulously wealthy. She told everybody that she had a wonderful marriage. It certainly enabled her to live in immense luxury. She didn't tell her close friends that her husband enjoyed extramarital affairs. He had made it clear to her that he liked sex with other women and said it was his prerogative. 'If you want to keep to this style of living,' he said, 'you had better keep the matter to yourself.' She succeeded for years.

One night, Tracy's friend spotted her husband fondling a young woman in his car. She told Tracy. Sorrow, rage and despair overwhelmed her. She felt utterly humiliated. It took medication, therapy, and a long and painful divorce before she got herself back together. 'I've been living a lie,' she said. 'It's never been all right with me.' We can pretend we're enjoying ourselves when it's not true. We try to convince ourselves and others how well our lives are going. Painful public deceptions and uncontrollable outbursts of anger are a common result.

We may decline to reveal the truth as an act of compassion for others. We may have to obscure our intentions and motivations. In such circumstances there is no violation of these ethical guidelines. Nevertheless we must take great care whenever there is even the mildest form of deviation from the truth of a situation. The wise have the capacity to take full responsibility for speaking the truth and for speaking less than the truth. In the latter case our words must be concise, revealing only the minimum.

I was asked to take a package of information to a respected political leader in a Third World country. A dissident group, working to overturn a military regime, showed me the information. I read it through and agreed with the content, so I said I would be a courier. The group was working to re-introduce democracy to their homeland. If the regime had not been clinging to power, it would have appreciated the efforts of this thoughtful group. The dissidents believed in constructive engagement and non-violent resistance. At the air ticket desk, I was asked whether I was carrying anything on behalf of anybody else. I said, 'Everything belongs to me.' I entered the country as a tourist. I was not searched. I passed over the large brown envelope to the leader's personal secretary as requested. It was a situation where I was economical with the truth.

If we kept to the strict letter of this ethical guideline, we would hardly have the opportunity to serve the needs of others. If there is a deception we may have to take the consequences. It is vital that we take care with language, communication and honesty. This enables us to walk a straight path in life and maintain genuine integrity. We must be diligent and skilful.

Sometimes we make promises but fail to keep the agreement. We are then accused of breaking promises, being unreliable and lying. Such accusations can hurt. We are not liars if we do not intend to lie, but we skirt the edge of lying when we keep letting people down. It becomes clear to us that, like everything else, a lie is not a self-existent thing but relates to everything else. There is a certain conceit when we believe that what we say is the truth, the whole truth and nothing but the truth. We realise that in the world of language there is no such thing as the complete truth.

We mostly base our perceptions on a combination of factors. These include memory, conditioning and beliefs. We consider the content of what we say and the consequences. This makes us vigilant concerning gossip, backbiting, exaggerations and gross generalisations.

We see that the world of language, true or false, fact or fiction, accurate or not, belongs to the field of sentient life. We have the opportunity to bring full awareness to communication. Embracing the duality of *I* and *other*, we stay steady. Our words must spring from an all-embracing and comprehensive wisdom.

INQUIRY

1. *Do you ever hide painful information from a person?*
2. *Do you always reveal painful information?*

3. Do your words depend upon what you imagine the other person's response will be?

4. Do you always have the right to make judgements about keeping silence?

5. What does it mean to be economical with the truth?

6. Do truth and lies make a fundamental difference to things?

Not Heedlessly Engaging in Alcohol or Drugs

When I flew into a Mediterranean country to give teachings, two friends greeted me at the airport and asked me if I would go directly with them to the apartment of a young woman. Her boyfriend had recently abandoned her. She had been pregnant. Four days before she had had an abortion. two days after that she had attempted suicide through taking an overdose of drugs: it was obvious that she had bottled up a great deal of agony and then consumed half a bottle of aspirin to escape the pain. When I met with her we talked about life, change, emotional outlets, the past, and fresh beginnings. When I left the country eight days later, she brought a huge jar of fresh olives to the airport for me. It was a very touching gesture.

We need to understand the personal and social problems of drugs, alcohol and tobacco rather than blindly condemn the people who use them. We also need to hold accountable those who exploit the vulnerabilities of people around addictive substances. There is a common view that this fifth Precept only applies to alcohol and illegal substances. Strictly speaking the Precept applies to addiction to any substance that contributes to *heedlessness*.

We are in danger of taking away some of our natural resources for dealing with recovery from illness. We have become such a speedy culture that we have lost the patience to wait or work for the health of the body to renew itself. We rarely look into the causes that make us feel unwell. Headaches, stomach problems, aches and pains, sleeplessness, weight gain: we quickly resort to the Western approach to health, namely attack and destroy. Our mantra in the West is 'I want to be cured. And when do I want it? I want it now.' Heedless of awareness, patience and skilful means, we opt for the quick and easy approach. We rush to the pharmacist for drugs because we have no practical remedies to turn to.

Another legal substance is tobacco, the most addictive and dangerous substance readily available. There are few deaths that are so long and agonizing as death from cancer caused by smoking. We can buy cigarettes anywhere, any time, in easily affordable numbers and compact boxes. The industry that produces these drugs ranks as one of the most successful at destroying the health and existence of its customers. It makes huge profits world-wide at the expense of addicts. Companies ruthlessly and heedlessly pursue their aim to get as many addicted as possible, persuading young people to become addicts as older addicts die. Every year huge numbers of people die long, slow, terrifying deaths from smoking-related diseases.

We live in a culture of individualism, and which embraces the formidable might of the corporate world. On average an advertisement assaults our senses every three minutes of our lives. It is hardly surprising that we find ourselves trapped in the loop. We work in the private or public sector to make money to buy goods and services from the private and public sector. Both sectors keep telling us what we must do, what we must have and where we must go. We obscure the reality of the cycle through the language of choice and individualism. Is it any wonder that we are heedless? Is it any wonder that alcohol, drugs, tobacco and medication become the escape for many from our mind-numbing secular life?

It is not enough to be in a counselling programme for alcoholics. It is not enough to try to give up smoking and gambling. It is not enough to give up taking drugs such as marijuana and Ecstasy for recreational use. We need organisations to challenge those who exploit us. We need to bring everything out into the open, make addictive substances legal and work inwardly and outwardly for change. We must hold accountable those who make profit at the expense of health.

The essential practice of the fifth Precept is learning to guard the sense doors. It is the willingness to be vigilant. If we slip off our guard for only one moment, it can be the first step on a slippery downhill slope to misery and hellishness. The urge from within to constantly gratify ourselves with a substance converts momentary pleasure into long-term pain. The unsatisfactory consequences far exceed the satisfaction. No amount of reasoning and solid argument seems able to persuade some users to desist from heedless activity born from association with various substances.

Of the Five Precepts or ethical guidelines, abuse of the fifth is common in triggering abuse of the other four. People make all manner of unskilful and destructive decisions under the influence of intoxication. There are people who later wished they had put their hand in the fire rather than upon the bottle, the needle, the pill, or the cigarette.

My father, a good man, had smoked since the age of twelve. As an adult he smoked ten to fifteen cigarettes per day. By the time he was in his sixties, he experienced the full impact of this addiction. The family tried to hide cigarettes from him – to no avail. In the last months before he died, he could barely walk. He couldn't catch his breath. He needed the support of the wall or a chair. One day a neighbour told my mother that she had seen my father slowly, painfully, walking up the street, mostly leaning on garden walls. At first he denied it. Then finally he admitted he was trying to make his way up the hill to the tobacconist five hundred metres from our home. He died from his addiction a few weeks later.

Inquiry

1. *Addictive patterns often make a mockery of choices and resolutions. What initial steps are necessary to let go of them?*

2. *Ending addiction may invite suffering in the period of transition. Are you willing to go through it? What resources are available to support you?*

3. *What support can you give to others struggling with their unhealthy patterns?*

4. *To be free from addictive patterns requires skilful means for wise goals. What are they?*

5. *Motivation, motivation, motivation. The power of motivation. So?*

FOUR
DIVINE ABIDINGS

Just as we can show love, God is all loving.
Just as we can show knowledge, God is all knowing.
Just as we can show power, God is all powerful.
Just as we can show energy, God is all energy.
Just as we can show generosity, God is all giving.
Just as we can be creative, God is all creativity.

Introduction

Through prayer, meditation, service, and spiritual knowledge, Hindus bring God closer to themselves. The Buddha departed from this form of relationship. He let go of the self's relationship to a God and instead explored the Middle Way. He said loving kindness, compassion, appreciative joy and equanimity are the Four Divine Abidings. Inner warmth in our feelings extended to all reveals the expansive heart. The teachings place much stress on this quality of feeling and its expression in daily life. This is what the Buddha regards as a truly Divine Abiding, not belief and identification with a metaphysical Divinity.

We do not have to involve ourselves in religious devotion, beliefs or rituals to experience the divine. Instead, we cultivate the opening of the heart. Such a practice enables us to live in an emotionally healthy way, to share our love and kindness with others. We thus break down any barriers of religious dogma, clinging and fixations, so that love and compassion shine through. We do not concern ourselves with a God either in language or vague intimation. Theism, agnosticism and atheism bear no relationship to the Dharma. It is the state of the heart that matters.

It can be remarkably difficult for religious people to understand each other when they give a different name to their God. They say much the same words, use much the same language, have similar buildings, and their books share similar values. Yet religious bigotry and subsequent divisions are common. It is not only among fundamentalists that this occurs. Anybody who believes that their faith is the only true teaching contributes to conflict. Nothing is truly worth holding on to or being identified with. In India, where religious tolerance has been advocated for more than three millennia, fanaticism and intolerance still occur.

The heart is the location for what is divine, nowhere else. In the heart's liberation, the vested interests of the self fade into obscurity.

Loving Kindness

Loving kindness holds more importance than all of our personal beliefs put together. Our social background matters little, nor what circles we move in. What matters is love. It has the power to reduce the lack of self-acceptance, egotism and harmful views.

Love is the genuine wish to contribute to the happiness and welfare of others. To love ourselves is to be respectful to ourselves every day. It is a major practice. We direct loving kindness everywhere, including to our whole being. There is an often repeated statement in the Buddhist tradition: 'sabbe satta sukita hontu'. This means simply, 'may all beings be happy'. Expressions of loving kindness are our major contribution to the happiness of others. What more can we do?

One expression of the loving mind is appreciation of the details of life, taking nothing and no one for granted. Knowing life is not long, we make our small acts count. Our life could end in a dark tunnel at any time. We cannot escape from the forces of existence, no matter how privileged we appear. We want life to be fair but it isn't. Life doesn't work under those rules. It functions and manifests according to the prevailing conditions.

There are times too when we hear of the beneficial changes that others are making in their lives. We hear of their insights, their acts of fearlessness, and their fresh creative initiatives. When others share this with us, they need to hear our support. Appreciation of others' acts ought to encourage us to examine our own lives. We do not have to live in the shadow of criticisms and arguments as though contention was healthy. If we remain narcissistic or cynical, the force of appreciation will remain stifled. We will be left with coldness in our heart and a mind frozen in its arrogance. It is all too easy simply to listen to thoughtful people with the occasional nod of the head.

Loving kindness serves as the antidote for negativity, whether gross or subtle. This practice of loving kindness serves as a sustained meditation that we purposely send out in all directions. It is panoramic in its scope. Once established, it naturally becomes free from ill will and the wish to undermine goodness and decency. Some may be suspicious of heartfelt people. If idealism is immature, it will not last. Under a wave of pressure love will slump into unhappiness and despondency.

Loving kindness is a translation from the Pali language of the word *metta*. This is associated at its root with *mitra*, which means 'friend'. This root can be seen in *Maitreya*, the name of the next Buddha – 'The Buddha of Loving Kindness or 'The Buddha of Deep Friendship'. Some Buddhists use *metta* meditation as an antidote for those who regard other forms of Buddhist meditation as dry. Authentic *metta* refers to the capacity to respond to the needs and rights of others. It may be helpful to ask yourself these questions:

INQUIRY

1. *What happens to you when the friendly become unfriendly?*

2. *What happens to you when others become cold and indifferent?*

3. *What happens to you when others engage in malicious speech, or plot to undermine you?*

4. *What happens when you feel nobody understands you?*

5. *What thoughts do you substantiate?*

6. *What thoughts serve as a basis for what you do next?*

We can compare the capacity of the practice of loving kindness to the stability of the earth. The earth gets treated frequently with great disrespect. We exploit it. We abuse it. But the earth absorbs all our mistreatment. The loving mind has the capacity to be similarly strong.

The loving mind brings direct benefits to the practitioner. We sleep well. We wake well. We do not experience horrible dreams. We are dear to others. We are dear to non-humans. The Buddha made a potent statement when he said we live to give *metta*. Both classical Buddhist texts and contemporary commentators share the same affirmation of *metta*.

It is all too easy to acquire a great deal of knowledge, a whole variety of mystical experiences and esoteric beliefs. But the true measure of our evolution as a human being shows in our *metta*. Through *metta* we get close to the Buddha mind. One sixth-century Buddhist commentary speaks of three kinds of people in the world – the friendly, the strangers, and the unfriendly. At times, we may have more association with one of these individuals or groups than another, or one person may appear as a friend, stranger or enemy.

PRACTICE

1. *Relax and get comfortable. Close your eyes and experience a warm, caring heartfulness towards others.*

2. *Be aware of the absence of ill will, desire to hurt, or hate in your heart.*

3. *Generate this warmth towards those who are in the immediate vicinity, including yourself, and those far away. Develop this meditation so that kindness of heart becomes firm and steady despite the vicissitudes of existence.*

4. *As you sit, gently repeat these words to yourself. You can also make up your own phrases or words that seem appropriate for you:*

   May my teachers, community, loved ones, friends and contacts be free from suffering and pain.

   May my mother and father be free from suffering and pain.

   May my brothers and sisters and relatives by free from suffering and pain.

   May my children and my grandchildren be free from suffering and pain. May people appreciate their interdependence with each other and their environment.

May animals and creatures in the earth, on the ground, in the air and under water live in safety and security.

May I abide with a warm heart and clear mind, and be free from pain.

May I contribute to the contentment, healing and insight of others.

May I be willing to take risks for their well-being.

May all beings know happiness. May all beings be supported. May all beings be free.

Compassion

I used to be a newspaper reporter. In 1969, I was working as a freelance reporter for ABC Radio in Sydney and was saving money to go back to Southeast Asia. I covered a story of a young man lost in the outback. He was missing for four days. Neither police, helicopters nor dogs could find him. An Aboriginal tracker did.

I returned to my small basement room in Kings Cross and turned on the radio to listen to the national news. After the lead items the newsreader read my report. Then a thought arose in my mind: 'Do I want to spend the rest of my life as the detached observer of other people's dramas?'

The following year I shaved my head, put on robes, took 227 precepts, and became a Buddhist monk in Thailand. I went for years without knowing the news of the world and felt that I didn't miss anything. I needed time to contemplate my existence. I needed to go deep enough to find out what mattered, if anything. I found out. Suffering matters. So does its resolution. Compassion comes from this awareness.

We are grateful for what we call the free press, but newspaper stories inspire only a tiny few to compassionate action. Proprietors, editors and reporters do their job for better or worse. We might inquire within ourselves why we read newspapers. Could we spend our time in more useful endeavours? It is one thing to know a lot about suffering as the major truth of life. It is something else to dedicate ourselves to another major truth, namely its resolution. Black print on white paper offers little assistance for that.

I remember when I was in the monastery I heard no news for the first three years. We were, of course, neighbours to Cambodia, Laos and Vietnam (then at war). We were also aware of local terrorism and the military's treatment of dissidents in the towns and villages surrounding our monastery. I didn't know about local politics. I didn't know the names of those in power or thrown out of power. I did not know the crime rate or the state of the economy. Our abbot and teacher took some of us regularly from the monastery to villages caught in conflict with the military or terrorists, in order to offer them support. In these villages we gave talks on morality, loving kindness and compassion.

Compassion comes through contact with the living, with those who suffer and those who work to resolve suffering. The printed word and the visual image is no substitute. Being better informed is no substitute for a response. We easily forget the world and its problems in the pursuit of information. Attachment to the news about suffering perpetuates it.

We may have to renounce our preoccupation with information and expose our consciousness to an unfiltered perception of the immediacy of life. We may have to starve the mind of words and language, fast the body, and expose ourselves to the wonder and tragedy of existence. Then perhaps from deep within, love and compassion can move through us. We may discover the ability to empathise with the circumstances of others less fortunate than ourselves.

As with loving kindness, there is the potential to cultivate the compassionate heart in meditation. We can transform our inner life for the welfare of others. We can associate with those who care deeply for others. Some of their qualities may rub off on to us.

We think of parents bringing up a handicapped child, not for a few years, but for decades. They sacrifice themselves to give one individual as warm and supportive a life as possible. We think of those who travel to lands where countless anti-personnel mines lie buried. Every day, men and women mindfully take one step after the next, clearing fields of these obscene instruments of war. The process is painstakingly slow: it can take weeks to clear a few fields. We think of the young people willing to bury themselves in tunnels beneath the earth or build houses in trees. They endure despite bitter weather to save one bit of earth from abuse. We think of the thousands of charities in Britain alone staffed by people who wish to make a contribution to the lives of others.

There may be egos involved in all of this. There may be the regularity and monotony of a routine. We could probably dredge up a few cynical attitudes if we wished towards such people – self-interest, nothing else better to do, a desire for acknowledgement, power, guilt, and so on. That may all be true, yet we can't forget their integrity of heart.

We may need to generate some time for meditation and reflection. To meditate means to be silent and still. It means attention to the depth of inner feelings of solidarity. In our silence we gain strength and determination to feel close to others. We see the apparent gap of separate existence as self-delusion.

We need to reflect on our relationship to life around.

We need to reflect on the conditions and causes of suffering.

We need to reflect on the route to the resolution of suffering.

We need to reflect on practical steps to resolve suffering.

This is our starting point for compassion. We train ourselves to keep the focus through the days and years. We are not ambitious. We are not trying to save the world. We have simply directed our life to what matters. We dedicate ourselves daily to living with wisdom and compassion. Like the two wings of a bird, we know that each wing gives support to the other.

INQUIRY

1. *What is the most significant act of compassion that you have honestly engaged in recently?*

2. *Do you need to get out of your comfort zone and expose yourself to the real world?*

3. *Do you understand that you don't have to go out of your front door to demonstrate a caring and compassionate life?*

4. *Have you tied yourself to a routine that inhibits wisdom of the heart?*

Appreciative Joy

Appreciative joy is like being in love. Heavenly. There is some-thing positively magical about the experience of happiness and joy. We can experience its sweetness emerging not only out of our heart but also out of our whole being. In its emergence, joy uplifts con-sciousness out of the mundane and the mechanical. It transcends the ordinary mind with its fixed views and repetitive daily activities. The Pali word is *mudita*. It refers equally to the joy aris-ing at the happiness of others and the joy of unselfish experiences.

We make an appalling sacrifice when we substitute pleasure for joy. We lose the recognition of the difference between the two. This confusion has consequences for ourselves, others and the earth. Pleasure arises from securing and gaining what we want. It can become addictive through repetition. Drugs, alcohol, gam-bling, chocolate, money, property, goods, power, and secret sex are no substitute for joy. Through habit and addiction the mind stays trapped in a cycle of pleasure and pain.

Appreciative joy is different. It opens up a different relation-ship to life. Through depths of meditation, renunciation, receptiv-ity and interest, we become exposed to joy about all things great and small. We love seeing others happy and healthy. The maxi-mum contribution that we can make to the arising of joy is an abid-ing sense of receptivity, interest and connection. The joy of appreciation is something precious and sweet. It comes unexpect-edly. It is witnessing the ordinary, the unusual and the mystical. It is the joy at seeing the happiness and contentment of others. We love to see others bright, healthy, insightful and free. We truly nourish our life through such experiences. Such a joy comes through learning, association, love and humility.

Appreciative joy seems to emerge most easily and effectively from that which we cannot own and possess. On one of those long, warm, lingering summer days, we observe children playing with a balloon in the park. They are running around, jumping up and down, keeping the balloon in the air. They are not our children. We know the experience is momentary. We didn't come to the park looking for such an experience. It just arose in the natural scheme of things. We experience a joy at their playfulness, at their running up and down, as the balloon floats across the park.

In wintertime, we wake up in the morning and pull the curtain open. Unexpectedly, it has snowed. We open our bedroom window and we see a white, white world. We look at the rooftops, the branches of the trees, the cars. White pervades everywhere. It is breathtaking. We had no idea when we went to bed what we would wake up to. Naturally, we respond with joy. We experience a sense of awe and wonder. We leave it to the poets to struggle to find the words to communicate what we witness. The magic of the season is upon us and words seem empty to the immediacy of the response.

We are at the railway station. It is rush hour and we are hurrying along with the rest of humanity. The day is over. We have left the office, the factory or the classroom. Suddenly, we bump into an old friend whom we haven't seen for years. Strangely enough, a few odd thoughts about this person arose only the previous day. Then suddenly there she is – in the flesh. We are amazed. We hug. There is laughter, joy and recollection. We exchange telephone numbers and addresses. We determine to meet again soon. What a coincidence, we think to ourselves. We are overjoyed. We sit on the crowded train and our mind keeps going back to that meeting and the events of the decade or two since the last meeting. The world is full of the unexpected. It is much more common than the expected.

When we experience something that touches our heart, our mind can come in far too quickly to start describing the experience to ourselves or others. Or we move on to something else. We do not give ourselves the opportunity to feel the fullness of the joy within. The depth of appreciative joy then fades. We never give inner happiness the opportunity to flow through our being and so we are left only with a memory. The cynic might say: 'You're telling us to sit around all day doing nothing waiting for joy to appear.' In a life short of joy, the cynic's attitude attempts to dimiss this feature of the inner life instead of dismissing cynicism and the negative mind.

The cultivation of receptivity means keeping our eyes and ears open and focused. It means appreciating the importance of a heartfelt interest in what is around us and within us. The pre-condition for love, compassion and appreciative joy is the unmistakable sense of connection. Let us never forget it.

There are probably few teachings on earth that emphasise the importance of the heart as much as the Buddha's. He didn't encourage the pursuit of mystical experiences. He had scant regard for worship, offerings, prayers and various other religious indulgences. He understood why people took up such activities but he doubted whether they were conducive to liberation. Rites, rituals and ceremonies can dull the mind once the novelty has worn off. They inhibit the experience of natural joy that comes from being alive. For a free spirit, religious life can offer joy, but when we identify with a form, dogma or ideology it can also kill the spirit.

Dharma teachings do not proclaim any Omnipotent, Omnipresent, Omniscient Figure. Nor do they expect the individual to rely on himself or herself to overcome the grief, sorrow and lamentation that can arise. The resolution of any form of anguish rests in wisdom. The presence of wisdom, within or without, provides enormous solace to the human heart. It brings its own joy.

We find such happiness within ourselves, in others, nature, a book, or the flow of circumstances. We come across resources that make a real difference, genuinely contributing to living life wisely. We are grateful for those resources. It can help immensely to make sense of things, no matter how hopeless they might appear to be. All of this brings its own joy. It would be worthwhile making time and space to put aside the all-too-familiar so that we become truly conscious human beings. We can experience joy through contact with the teachings in their various manifestations. The practice of empathetic joy overcomes jealousy at the loss of somebody's love or envy of another person's success.

Our hearts have the capacity to release a tremendous amount of joy. It is as though our self has to get out of the way for that to happen. Whether that joy arises in meditation or in the unexpected moment, we know it touches us in a deep place. Its benefits can heal the most wounded soul.

INQUIRY

1. *What do you have to change or renounce to taste a heartfelt joy?*
2. *What brings joy?*
3. *What touches deeply?*

4. *Do you experience joy for others and in solitude?*
5. *What do you have to be grateful for?*
6. *What are the ways that you share your joy with others?*

Equanimity

By any standard, she was beautiful. In her late teens she had married a man in his early thirties. Her intuition told her that his attention went frequently towards another woman he had known for years. There was already a great deal of pressure in her life. By her mid-twenties she was suffering an eating disorder. She pulled herself through a crisis period and found great strength as a result. Religion told her to forgive the woman and the deceptions of her former husband. That was a tall order for anybody. She finally understood the wisdom of equanimity towards the past through deliberately moving on. She made small resolutions and kept to them until she built up her inner strength. Rightly, she valued this equanimity as much as forgiveness. It enabled her to get on with her life. She knew her heart was in the right place.

It is not unusual to highlight love, compassion and joy in the religious life. Equanimity has not received the same attention. There are situations in life where it can be too much to ask ourselves to forgive another. We can make demands upon our emotional life far beyond our capacity. It is an unreasonable expectation to imagine we can show an unbroken flow of love and kindness. The force of equanimity and its very presence reminds us of our humanity. Non-attachment and non-clinging matter as much as love.

We have to learn to remain equanimous in the presence of what life offers. In family situations we need every drop of equanimity to cope with the ups and downs of issues between family members. There is often a compelling need for people to find fault with loved ones. The joke that Christian humorists like to make is, 'God gave us our friends, the Devil gave us our relatives.' One of the important factors for equanimity is integrity. When we lose our equanimity we sink to the level of others. Under the spell of the storyline, we become as resentful and selfish as those we condemn.

The practice of equanimity enables us to rise above the turmoil and wrangling of others. Others will bring upon themselves far more suffering than our ill will towards them. There is little point in launching into vitriolic attacks upon others. Acting as prosecutor, judge and jury shows little understanding of a situation. Our mindset might be extraordinarily close to the mind-set we are condemning. To stay equanimous is to keep our peace.

Several hundred years ago a marauding general and his army were conquering one of the Buddhist countries. He arrived at the entrance to a Buddhist monastery and demanded to see the abbot. He stared at the abbot and said to him, 'I am the leader of this army.' Then picked up his huge sword, held it above the head of the abbot and said to him, 'I can cut you in half without blinking an eyelid.'

The abbot looked him straight in the eye, bowed, and said, 'I am a Buddhist monk. I can be cut in half without blinking an eyelid.' Successive generations of Buddhist monks and serious lay practitioners of the Dharma love this story, which conveys the inner power of equanimity: the capacity to stay steadfast in the face of an immediate threat. That doesn't come easily. We practise in our meditations to stay steady in the face of pain. We practise to be able to face change and uncertainty with steadfast equanimity. The teachings pay respect to equanimity as much as to love, compassion and joy.

Critics claim that Westerners are trying to engage in something unfamiliar and unnatural to them when they meditate in the cross-legged posture. In my observation, pain arises in the body and problems in the mind for Easterners as well as Westeners. Meditation does not come easily for any particular culture. It is not unusual in such a practice to extend the period of meditation. The capacity to sit still in meditation can develop from a few minutes to hours. Images of the Buddha serve as a reminder to sit still, to be utterly aware and present to whatever comes.

With quiet determination, we observe whatever sensations and experiences arise and dissolve in body and mind. We learn to embrace without fear or tension the diversity of these experiences. We learn not to cling to the range of pleasurable experience and not to avoid the unpleasant ones. The development of this skill and understanding becomes a wonderful resource in daily life.

Under pressure from within or without, we see our thoughts can undermine equanimity. If we allow thoughts to take a grip on consciousness we get caught up in all manner of mind-states. Under the compelling influence of such tendencies, we lack the capacity to handle situations skilfully. If we recognise this in ourselves, then we need to develop equanimity to thoughts. We practise not grasping them as a statement of reality.

A friend's practice of mindfulness of breathing that she learnt on retreats naturally arose to give her support in a moment of threat. Late one night, a man accosted her near her home. He grabbed her from behind, put a knife to her throat and demanded her handbag. Such a situation can be someone's worst nightmare. She told me that she remained extraordinarily quiet as he made this demand in her ear.

Surprisingly, the first words that came out of her mouth to him were in the form of a question, 'Do you think this is a good idea?' The man, obviously under intense pressure and excitement, let her go, calling her crazy. We often don't realise our capacity to be equanimous in the face of circumstances. We cannot rely upon hope that we will be able to deal with what life offers us today, or tomorrow, or on the last day of our existence. Development of equanimity acts as an important contribution to our welfare. It is a challenge and a test.

The two biggest challenges to a grounded equanimity are attraction and aversion. We can be pushed and pulled about by these two forces. For example, absence of equanimity at times of sexual attraction can play havoc with our lives. The pull towards a third person can result in destroying years of a personal relationship. The outcome of a few minutes of pleasurable sex can result in months, if not years, of disruption and anguish for ourselves and others. We allow ourselves to get sucked into compromising situations that we regret afterwards. Even at the time, the thought can arise that this is madness, but the force of attraction is too strong. It then seems grossly unfair that the price for a little pleasure is so much pain. Equanimity matters as much as all positive human emotions. It is a safeguard enabling us to live with peace of mind.

INQUIRY

1. *Where do you experience the least equanimity?*

2. *In what way can you develop equanimity towards this?*

3. *Is it possible to feel equal towards both pain and the pursuit of pleasure?*

4. *We apply equanimity towards what* arises, *what* stays *and what* passes. *What is your relationship to what arises, what stays and what goes?*

5. *What kind of responses occur in you when you reflect upon these three faces of existence?*

FOUR
ABSORPTIONS

All beings love the warmth of happiness,
Like sunlight to a field's sunflowers,
For inside this depth, peace is found
In meditation of a fragrant hour.

Introduction

The Four Absorptions are:

1. Inner happiness.
2. Sublime joy.
3. Equanimity.
4. Neither pleasure nor pain.

They are specialised meditation practices emphasising various depths of happiness, joy, and equanimity. They are not directly concerned with gaining insight, though that may happen, particularly in the First Absorption. Through the depth of these Absorptions, we experience an extraordinary sense of inner well-being. These Absorptions are not a withdrawal from the world. They give exceptional support and stability to the deepest levels of the mind.

The Absorptions contribute to purifying the mind from the poisons (to use a word of the Buddha) of greed, hate and self-delusion. They help dissolve the influence of the Five Hindrances. Through depths of meditation we taste inner happiness. The quality of this happiness diminishes the appetite for feeding these

188

Hindrances. Through the experience of the Absorptions we become less demanding of the world. Our deep inner joy and peace contribute to peace in the world. The way to peace is via inner peace.

It is not necessary to describe these Absorptions as a religious experience. The Four Absorptions are the natural outcomes of silence, stillness, focused attention and the response of happiness. Going from the First Absorption to the Second, Third and Fourth is going deeper at every level.

First Absorption – Inner Happiness

As a teacher of the two primary forms of meditation, namely calm and insight, I receive regular letters from enthusiastic retreatants. They tell me they have experienced the benefits of both kinds of meditation and wish to devote more time in their lives to meditation.

The experience of meditation reveals not only its significance but also its potential. There is access to a depth of happiness and contentment in meditation that not only serves ourselves, but causes us to place fewer demands upon others and the world. Inner calm and a focused attention enable the arising of a sublime joy to suffuse our cells, emotions and thoughts. There are various conditions conducive to such depths of experience. They include:

1. A teacher who knows these experiences intimately for himself or herself. He or she acts as a guide for calm and insight meditation.

2. The methods and techniques that enable the depth to occur.

3. A suitable environment where silence and support for depth is encouraged.

4. The willingness to dedicate oneself to going deep.

We also need to consider a nutritious diet, exercise for flexibility, and a daily routine. A suitable posture allows the whole body to relax and yet remain straight, whether we sit with a straight back, cross-legged, or use a wooden stool or chair. We then turn our attention to the breathing process. We develop calmness through consciously experiencing inhaling and exhaling. Through this practice, the brain cells gradually become settled. We feel rested in the present moment. There is no wish in the mind to be anywhere else. When discomfort arises in the body we stay with it, moving only occasionally and returning to the original posture.

Over the days, we gradually extend our sitting time, and as our depth of meditation develops, we experience feelings of deep happiness emerging from the calmness. Initially we may decide to induce happiness *deliberately* through bringing to mind what we love or cherish through an image or memory. After some period of practice, this technique becomes unnecessary as the experience of joy and effortlessness suffuses the whole body. We experience bliss, strong or subtle, pervading us from our head to our toes. Each breath becomes a breath of joy, a breath of happiness. The firmness and uprightness of the body keeps us grounded so that we don't blissfully space out. As we get proficient in the practice, we become thoroughly absorbed into this inner, concentrated happiness. This is called the First Absorption.

We can then abide effortlessly in a field of extraordinary well-being. Joy fills consciousness and affects all our senses. We also experience two types of reflection in the midst of this joy. First, reflective thought contributes to establishing the consciousness with the experience of the First Absorption. It might be appreciation for the experience itself. Second, discursive thought contributes to insight and understanding of the experience. Owing to the depth, these thoughts clearly reflect situations.

Through practice and mastery of the skill in such Absorption, we realise a depth of happiness and peace not dependent on our environment. (This Absorption is known as the First *Jhana* in Buddhism.) This capacity to journey deep within takes us beyond the troubling influence of our attachments, that are bound up in the personality structure of our likes and dislikes.

For many, there is bound to be an interest and attraction towards the Four Absorptions of happiness, joy, equanimity and neither pleasure nor pain. Yet we need to be careful since, without realising, we can get into a degree of desire and will-power to achieve these goals. We then forget that the force of desire and use of will-power creates pressure on the mind. Instead of absorption into happiness, we get absorbed into hellish states of mind.

Each of the Four Absorptions is a meditation practice. For some people the Absorptions come easily, often through other kinds of meditation. For others, they arise spontaneously or through continuity and commitment to depth of calmness practice. Despite their best intentions, not everybody reaches such depths. That does not mean to say such people have blocks or unresolved problems. It may simply indicate that the inner formations are simply not conducive. The presence of suitable conditions, inner and outer, makes the greatest contribution to allowing these joyful depths to arise within.

A regular, daily meditation practice and mindful, stress-free living can make access to the Four Absorptions possible. If the mind is agitated or there are bodily pains to attend to, then the focus is primarily mindfulness, development of calmness, clarity and insight into the current process, not trying to enter into Absorptions. It is also not necessary to withdraw from the so-called 'real world' to the monastery for these practices.

PRACTICE

(Twice a day, around forty minutes per session.)

1. *Sit with straight back and take long slow in and out breaths for a ten-minute period. Relax on each outbreath. (Be careful not to hyperventilate.)*

2. *Feel for ten minutes the aliveness of the whole body with a calm abiding.*

3. *Recite slowly in the mind for ten minutes such phrases as:*

   May I be filled with happiness.

   May I be filled with joy.

   May I be filled with contentment.

   May I be filled with peace.

   May others benefit from this meditation.

4. *Allow ten minutes for the whole being to rest, upright, relaxed and comfortable. Remain single-pointed and present to the sense of depth of sublime pleasant feeling in the body.*

5. *Be patient. Don't place pressure upon yourself to achieve these Absorptions. With practice, happiness will begin to emerge from the depth of your being.*

Each of the Absorptions is a wonderful contribution to health and happiness. They are not the consummation of the depths of meditation or spiritual practice, no matter how deep the happiness and joy. To settle for any one of the Four Absorptions would be to settle for something less than the best. The conditioned is no substitute for enlightenment and realising the unconditioned.

Second Absorption – Sublime Joy

We have this remarkable capacity to be aware, to see deeply into things, even to see into timelessness. We also have this terrible capacity to hook ourselves into the ordinary and transient and place our hopes and fears upon what our senses perceive. It is a mistake, and we pay a terrible price for it. The result is suffering and anxiety. It doesn't have to be like that. The Four Absorptions remind us of our heart's natural capacity for joy – just as much as the eyes have the capacity to see and the ears to hear.

In the Second Absorption there is also the fading away of interest in the pursuit of pleasure of the senses. That pleasure seems gross compared to the joy arising out of Absorptions. There is a further refinement from the First Absorption to the Second: it is a significant shift of experience. In the Second Absorption, all thoughts, reflective and discursive, cease. This may appear a small refinement. In fact, it brings a significant qualitative difference to the depth of meditation. Refinement of happiness produces a sublime joy. There is an exceptional sense of calmness and oneness of mind. The heart feels suffused with delight. The depth of contrast between the First and Second Absorption is remarkable.

Sublime happiness, joy and serenity, with the presence of *samadhi*, establish the Second *Jhana*. There is a non-conceptualised appreciation of experience in the last three Absorptions.

How long can an Absorption last?

This depends upon inner qualities, power of attention, lucidity and level of energy. It can be for a few minutes, hours, through the night, or longer.

Are these Absorptions like a trance?

No. Trance cannot offer the depth of *samadhi*. Absorption arrests the various Hindrances that affect our lives. In Absorptions one is clearly present.

Can I come out of any Absorption at any time?

Yes. Absorption is not at the expense of awareness and clarity. One may have to leave the Absorption to interact with the world. This movement from deep absorption to activity does not necessarily sacrifice the joy, happiness and deep sense of well-being. That is the wonderful thing about these Absorptions. They are not self-indulgent. Their benefits suffuse the senses.

Why does such a state of Absorption end?

The Absorption ends for a variety of reasons. Energy fades. A surrounding event breaks the Absorption as it strikes one or more of the senses. Pain in the body or an unresolved issue can cut through the absorption.

Upon the fading away of the absorption am I thrown into the world of Hindrances?

Not necessarily. You may simply be relaxed and quietly alert. Unresolved issues, patterns and addictions can lose their grip on consciousness. One can emerge out of them feeling utterly refreshed and left wondering what happened to all of these so-called personal problems. Or you may see that you have issues that need attention

Could I get stuck in one of these Absorptions?

No, even if it seems attractive. You can only get stuck in the memory. An Absorption has its own sweetness and vibration to it. It contributes to inner healing and harmony.

Could I get so attached to this kind of depth of experience that I lose love and compassion for others?

Yes. Nothing whatsoever is worth getting attached to. One must be vigilant after these experiences. Clinging to them makes access to Absorptions that much more difficult. It usually requires humility and sensitivity to go deep.

Some of the mystics write about being drunk on God, soaked in ecstasy or awash with the Divine. These experiences, wonderful and ecstatic as they are, belong to the 'highs' of consciousness. They are not necessarily meditative Absorptions. I remember sitting in the Himalayas with a God-filled Hindu sage. As we looked out across those awesome mountains, he turned to me and asked, 'What do you see?' I replied with my heart, 'The Truth that is Immeasurable.' The swami got out of his cross-legged position, stood up and yelled across the valley, '*I see God everywhere!*' He then sat down, closed his eyes with that look of divine bliss that Hindu yogis love so dearly and went into meditation. No wonder all swamis have at the end of their name *ananda* (which means 'bliss'). Absorptions are not a high but a depth. The swami loved the heights as much as the depths.

The element of space suffuses this high while the element of earth suffuses depth. In this Second Absorption, joy and happiness reveal the inner treasure of the heart. The experience remains free from indulgence in sense-door activity, acts of devotion or emotive beliefs. It is of a different order with its own mystery, free from thought and religious language. It neither affirms nor denies anything spiritual or religious.

Third Absorption – Equanimity

A yogi asked the Buddha to describe his normal state of mind. The Buddha described the Third Absorption. He said he dwelt mindful and clearly conscious. At this level there is a depth of equanimity and a further stabilising of the mind. In the Third Absorption we experience deep peace. This peace is not easily knocked away through surrounding circumstances. It means that the ebb and flow of events upon the senses fails to disturb us. There is a capacity to abide in deep equanimity. There is a steadfastness, calmness and clarity with a genuine quality of presence. In the Third Absorption happiness arises directly from this deep contentment.

Buddhist texts refer to it as abiding in a 'fine material sphere'. There are no signals whatsoever of restlessness, agitation or unsettledness. The brain cells remain impeccably still; the body knows no agitation. There is no demanding anything from oneself nor others.

It is not unusual in this Absorption as well as the others to interpret the experience in ultimate terms, but Absorptions are not ultimate experience. Insight (Vipassana) meditation serves as an invaluable preparation for the Four Absorptions and vice versa. These invaluable meditations often get neglected in the Buddhist training. The cultivation of mindfulness through formal training makes an excellent preparation for *Jhanas*. If we know ourselves well, we will know the difference between effort and striving, patience and resignation, depth of peace and the superficially quiet mind.

We can often have peaceful moments in our day yet hardly be aware of the fact. This is the most superficial form of peace of mind. It doesn't take much to blow it away. Bringing an alert presence to these quiet moments allows a gradual and organic deepening of the quiet moment into a depth of peace. Obviously we can't push this quiet moment deep within, but we can allow it to sink deeper. It is an alert and undemanding presence that is the key to making this possible.

Can I go straight to the Third or Fourth Absorption without experiencing the previous ones?

Yes. Absorptions can take place gradually – One, Two, Three, Four – or suddenly. It can happen that a meditator experiences the Third Absorption without exposure to the bliss and joyfulness of the first two Absorptions.

What do I need to do to gain mastery over the Jhanas?

Practise in a suitable environment. There is no substitute. There are those who enter quickly and easily into such experience and those who travel slowly. They are all making the journey into depth. Personal emotional history is not necessarily a significant factor. For some, insight and understanding of meditation and states of mind may have to come before Absorption meditations.

Could I suddenly find myself in one of these Absorptions and be unable to function?

No. It would be a contradiction in terms to make a problem out of an Absorption.

Isn't there a danger that I could become infatuated with this experience? If my mind stops still and there is no suffering in those periods, would I want to face the Three Characteristics of Existence?

Yes, there is a danger. Whatever we genuinely commit ourselves to involves a risk. If we get attached to these Absorptions, we will resist other experiences. There is a danger, and it is a serious one, of neglecting the capacity to witness existence, to investigate it. Becoming identified with and grasping on to any Absorption shows a lack of understanding. Insight meditation then needs to be cultivated.

How will I know the difference between this depth of peace and liberation?

Liberation knows no measurement. The world of birth and death shrinks in its significance. When one is liberated, there is the capacity to see through the mind with its varying depths. Nothing is held on to anywhere. One knows one is free – like a bird that leaves no pathways in the sky. Liberation embraces the deep and the shallow.

In the Third *Jhana* stillness is a key element for deep equanimity. Stillness of body, stillness of mind and stillness of inner reaction. The world of events loses its power to buffet the mind around. We experience a realm of great silence.

Fourth Absorption – Neither Pleasure nor Pain

Pleasure and pain play a major part in our life. It seems like a cruel quirk of nature that we spend so much time involved in these two fields of experience. We live in a world where there is the apparent potential to get everything we want and to satisfy the senses. There is equally the potential to suffer indescribably over what we have.

In the Fourth Absorption we know a depth of experience that falls into neither of those two categories. We know through direct experience what it means to overcome pleasure and pain. These opposites of life dissolve in the depths of being. The capacity to abide in this Absorption makes it harder for the potential for conflicting opposites to hold sway over consciousness.

Pain consists of sensations taking place in the body that give the mind trouble. We tell ourselves that we need pain as the body's means to tell us something is wrong physically. In this commonly held view, pain becomes vital to the human organism and to our experience. The hard truth is that pain doesn't always tell us that we need to move or do something.

Numerous people experience various pains and still do nothing about them. Messages are coming out of the body but the mind is ignoring, denying or underestimating their significance. There are others who at the first sign of pain fear the worst. It sends the mind into anxious thinking. Pain then becomes the vehicle for worry. As the unpleasant body sensations ripple through the psyche the mind can then begin to panic or fight the wave of sensations. Without equanimity, we can lose all balance in the face of the pleasurable and the painful.

One of the important features of a clear mind is the ability of awareness to mirror what is happening. Out of this capacity, we can respond wisely, free from the notion of pain terrorising our life. The Fourth Absorption carries the capacity to purify the mind through this equanimity. Not caught up in pleasure or pain, grief or joy, we stay grounded and deeply centred. This Absorption stands beyond attraction and aversion, likes and dislikes. We remain intimately connected with the present.

There are times in our life when every minute we have given to Dharma teachings and practices will have been worthwhile. Every moment of exposure can become a resource at a future point in our life. In difficult situations, the hours of calm and insight meditation become worth their weight in gold.

Our practice and training in this *Jhana* may have occurred in the supportive environment of a retreat centre, monastery, cave or at home. Wherever we go in this world the mind accompanies us – for better or worse. Out of the experience of the Four Absorptions, we feel their support in daily life. They become a resource. The Buddhist texts refer frequently to the importance of the Four Absorptions and the Four Divine Abidings. The former concerns the depth of inner experience through meditation. The latter concerns the depth of the heart's relationship to others.

The experience of the Fourth Absorption reveals the importance of knowing that which is beyond pleasure and pain. When pleasure and pain arise in the fire of daily circumstances, we will have the opportunity for a balanced perspective on them. We will appreciate all the training we undertook to develop the Four Absorptions. The wisdom and common sense of such meditation practices will be very clear.

FOUR FORMLESS
REALMS

What sweet depths echo in this life
That lead to discovery! Yet never far away,
For where can we go but to humble origins?
Nothing offers itself to be attended to
Yet there abides this infinite expanse.

Introduction

The Four Formless Realms are:

1. Realm of infinite space.
2. Realm of infinite consciousness.
3. Realm of infinite nothingness.
4. Realm of neither perception nor non-perception.

Each of them reveals an authentic reality different from the conventional one of self in the world. As with the Four Absorptions, each of these deep formless experiences is a refinement of the one that comes before. They are generally only available through meditation but can occur spontaneously. Authentic experience of the Formless Realms can never be artificially induced since they require depth of being and refinement of consciousness.

To enter into one of these Realms is breathtaking. One feels in touch with something awesome and expansive – far beyond the usual constrictions of the mind. These Realms are valid perceptions. The meditator who gains access to the Formless Realms doesn't forget them. They make an impression in the depths of the psyche.

Each one of them opens out one's world. They make one realise how much time is spent, if not wasted, in ordinary, conditioned perceptions. Along with our views and habitual patterns, we live with the conceit of believing we are always in touch with the real world. The Four Formless Realms don't indicate the attainment of liberation, nor indicate a Noble One, but they certainly help us to break out of conditionality. They make clear to us that there is more to reality than our conditioned considerations and the impact upon self of what goes on around us.

Realm of Infinite Space

I spent most of 1973 as a Buddhist monk living in a cave on the island of Ko Pnag Nga, off the coast of Thailand. The cave was situated on a ledge above the coconut trees, looking out over the sea. I had gone there from the insight meditation (Vipassana) monastery, Wat Chai Na in southern Thailand, where I had lived for more than three years. At that time I was the only Westerner living on this small tropical island.

I would get up before dawn, take my mat and sit on the ledge, looking out across the palm trees to the rising sun. I would observe the new day changing from darkness to light. No two days are ever the same. The new day brought with it colour, vibrancy and warmth. Afterwards, I would step out of my cross-legged posture, pick up my begging bowl, and slowly make my way down to the fishing village to go on the begging round.

In the evening, I sat cross-legged again, faced the opposite direction, and watched the sun set from light to dark. Again, no two sunsets are ever the same. There is a wonder in this unfolding of life. Most days I loved these hours. Occasionally it was an endurance test to follow it through, even though I had nothing else to do. But mostly, the heart cannot help responding with awe and wonder. I loved this solitude, where my companions were all non-human.

It would also happen that a sense of space impregnated itself upon my awareness. It became well established. That was all that I felt. I simply experienced the realm of infinite space. This realm accommodates everything imaginable. The realm of infinite space takes the form out of form, the thingness out of things. The body, which serves as a boundary between inner and outer, slips from consciousness. It is as if one did not exist. I knew life without myself. There was only this infinite expanse of space. And it felt fine.

These experiences alter consciousness long-term. They contribute to placing the minor events of life into a greater perspective. When there is genuine space in our lives, we are much less likely to get ensnared in the trivial and mundane. Our inner life can respond to the wisdom of such experiences. Outside liberation itself, the experience of the realm of infinite space makes the most substantial contribution to a spacious life. There is a tremendous sense of acknowledgement of how accommodating space is of all things. This is not a thought but a realisation.

There are three ways of employing the mind in meditation. One is directly focusing on a particular object such as the breath, body, sound. The second is meditating with an open awareness to include all objects equally – sounds, body sensations and thoughts – but without seizing upon any of them. The third is an expansive objectless awareness. There is simply a spacious abiding free from interest in the objects, whether a particular one or objects in general.

In the latter, meditative awareness begins to fuse itself with space. As this space element fuses with awareness, it expands. It is experienced as all-pervasive – in all directions, inner and outer. Because one is meditatively centred, there is no 'spacing out' or feeling adrift. The world of things, of items, gets absorbed into this infinite space. Objects, near and far, then share the same characteristic feature of belonging to space. We experience this space as limitless and all-accommodating.

If we are to taste such experiences, it is vital that we learn to travel lightly in our lives. Contact with these realms becomes difficult for those who grasp on to things and get preoccupied with notions of substantial ideas. These formless realms are available to those who combine renunciation with contemplation. It is the fusion of these two that makes all this possible.

These experiences may also occur within the context of the few days of a meditation retreat, or arise in the midst of the most ordinary everyday experience. The experience of infinite space may just become memory. For others the love of space grows significantly as a result. One loves the space between objects, the space that enables objects to be. One appreciates the space even in a crowded environment.

There is a deepening of aesthetic understanding of the relationship between form and space. If the experience of infinite space is genuine, the *I* does not make a big noise about it. Long-term benefits come naturally. We know what it means to live a spacious and undemanding life.

Realm of Infinite Consciousness

It easily happens that, though the experience of the Realm of Infinite Consciousness, we treat consciousness as supreme, as Consciousness with a capital 'C'. When the whole mind is very silent and still, energy is present. We are utterly attentive, utterly present in the here and now. The events of body and environment begin to soften. They become still. They serve as a background to Consciousness. There is an authentic sense that this functions as an extraordinary receptacle which enables us to witness the wonder of the night sky and a flower close at hand.

In this realm, the sense of 'I am', roles, identities, personal history, and our future fade. They become irrelevant as statements of who we are. Consciousness embraces everything, becoming the means through which the world reveals itself. We then experience it as our Highest Self, our True Self. No other element in the nature of things seems to affirm our presence so strongly. In this realm, Consciousness opens out beyond all its usual limiting reference points.

At the time, all of this acts as a remarkable revelation. We ARE Consciousness. Consciousness is Absolute. It would be tempting at this point to believe that we have discovered enlightenment. Our experience seems to confirm this, as well as what we have read in various sacred texts. We are tempted to believe that we have arrived at the consummation of the teachings. Some saints have implied that there is no further to go than this. Yet there is still more to experience and understand.

The experience of the Realm of Infinite Consciousness

becomes unmistakably, glaringly obvious. Instead of treating consciousness as an outcome of the evolutionary process, we give it a
central place. The movement of the mind that compares past to
present to future is simply a movement of the mind.

In this realm, we cannot locate Consciousness in the body or
outside it. We cannot make it an object of interest. Consciousness
reveals equally *I*, *my*, *self* and the world. It opens us to the vast field
of existence. There is the conviction of an Absolute Oneness,
beyond words. There is no limit to what Consciousness can
acknowledge. Therefore, we regard this Consciousness, this Pure
Awareness, the Self, as infinite. This perception gets thoroughly
well established as the primary reference point.

In the monastery, the Buddhist teacher sat in the front of the
monks and nuns. There was a palpable silence in the air. He was a
man of words and presence. The *Sangha* remained attentive to his
every word, his every gesture. With awareness, in this meditative
atmosphere, the teacher turned and slowly lifted his palms up
towards the ceiling. He said quietly and serenely, 'Consciousness,
consciousness, consciousness.' Nobody moved. It was as though
everybody present embraced a collective conscious presence. This
Infinite Consciousness absorbed one and all including the bare elements of existence. Everybody felt they had participated in a sacred
moment.

Once you have experienced this Consciousness, every
moment, every touch of life and the sheer diversity of things make
one see frequently its infinite capacity. These experiences are profound, rare and available. However, as with other experiences in
the Infinite Realms, there is still a very clear sense of going into the
experience and coming out of it. A deep meditative life can make
access much more easy and frequent. Whether rare or regular,
these experiences fade from perception. It is not that one needs an
act of will to achieve such experiences, nor another act of will to
get out of them. Energy fades, states of mind surface. If one could
abide permanently in such a state it would certainly indicate access
to a very deep experience but it would not be liberation. To imply
or claim this realm is supreme is a limited position.

We realise such a profound experience invites interpretations
of true reality. We give such experiences authority about the final
truth of things. Nevertheless, if some understanding has emerged

out of our experiences, the insights will have an impact on our relationship with the finite and the perishable. If no understanding comes about, then the experience of these realms will make no difference to our daily life.

In this Realm of Infinite Consciousness, there is also the potential to move effortlessly through heavens and hells, the sensual, material, mental and other realms. In the depths of these experiences, the physical body cannot restrict us. When we truly absorb into such a realm we understand that it has a greater force than the pull of materialism. Objects, near or far, apparent or hidden, get altered or exposed through the power of consciousness. Nevertheless, the Realm of Infinite Consciousness is not a final resting place.

The experience of Infinite Consciousness supersedes the Realm of Infinite Space. There is a clear and tangible knowing that Infinite Consciousness is a significant refinement of the previous realm of experience.

Realm of Infinite Nothingness

Superficially, the Realm of Infinite Nothingness sound like an anti-life experience. It is not unusual for the Buddhist tradition to be accused of promoting this view. Critics, including theologians and philosophers, will point to words used in the Buddhist tradition such as emptiness, suffering, not-self. They regard these words as examples of an anti-life view, and take issue with comments from some prominent Buddhists who speak of 'life as suffering'. All of this feeds the rejection of Buddhism.

The Realm of Infinite Nothingness is a realm of *not-something*. The word in the Pali language for 'nothingness' is *akincina*. *Kincina* means 'something'. *Akincina* literally means 'not something'. We have made contact with someone. Then he or she disappears out of our life. We get reminded that that event is now a non-event. We go from something to nothing, presence to absence. One makes the other possible.

We can meditate on the absence of something. We can go into this experience deeply and fully acknowledge it. We can enter this Realm of Nothingness without any associations whatsoever of horror or fear. We can welcome the Realm of Infinite Nothingness as an authentic feature of existence.

The items of existence, inner and outer, drop away. There is no notion of one thing being anything whatsoever. The experience of Infinite Nothingness makes clear the significance of absences. Presence gives rise to absence and absence gives rise to presence.

For some the experience of the Realm of Infinite Nothingness is a breakthrough. It acts as a major relief from the substance viewpoint. When we stop to look at the field of deep experience, we see things in a fresh way. On face value, Infinite Nothingness sounds as bleak as one could imagine. We hear Nature hates a vacuum. The reality is that Nature loves a vacuum. It is an important feature in nature. The previous Realm of Infinite Consciousness seems gross in comparison to the Realm of Infinite Nothingness. We see that even consciousness gets absorbed into this Infinite Nothingness.

We have all had the experience of attempting to observe a thought. We can't. The moment we try, the thought is no longer there. This is not the experience of Infinite Nothingness; it simply reminds us of our inability to fix thoughts. We see how much we live in a dream-world of deceptive thoughts and personal soap operas. Our thoughts can dominate our lives, even though they vanish upon direct observation.

As with the other Absorptions and Realms, it would be quite easy to put any of them into an ultimate category. Through inner development we gain mastery of these experiences. We come to love the experience of Infinite Nothingness. It holds no fear, no horror, nothing for the self to build on. In this Realm absolutely nothing is going on whatsoever. It is simply a Realm to enter and exit from, providing the stepping stone to a genuine liberation. Authentic liberation stands free from the experience of something and nothing. Formless experiences in the Four Infinite Realms fall short.

Realised ones appreciate immensely the Infinite Realms. They know they are not an end in themselves, but nor are they a dead-end. Dharma teachings fully acknowledge the benefit of Absorptions and the Infinite Realms. In the contemplative life each one is worthy of practice, exploration and understanding.

If we miss contact with others, we can't hide it. The mind will produce its own inner dialogues to compensate for external ones. If we love solitude and meditation, then these Realms of Infinite Experience lie within our scope. It would be a pity to pass through life not experiencing deeply the peace of *absence of*. This state of Infinite Nothingness gets revealed in the depths of meditation. Untying ourselves from the world of thoughts and things makes this important experience accessible. Death – absence of the known – then loses some of its terror.

This Realm contributes significantly to living with nothing and being nobody. We are not afraid of disappearances, things vanishing, or being separated from the familiar. The experience of the Realm of Infinite Nothingness produces gratitude. Absence of or dissolution of do not produce fear; they produce nothing. We see that though everything can be and will be taken away, we do not have to plunge into sorrow. We sense we are close to the truth of things. The self and the world bear no eternal features. This Realm can be a doorway to liberation. In liberation we see through the Realm of Something and Nothing.

Realm of Neither Perception nor Non-perception

The Fourth of these Infinite Realms is a refinement on the other three. It is the Realm of Neither Perception nor Non-perception. This realm of experience dissolves any perception of the substance of space, consciousness and nothingness.

In the depth of this experience we cannot assume a perception. It would be an extreme standpoint to assume that a perception occurs or that it does not occur. The subtle nature of this Realm makes the previous one seem gross. It is like going from a tricycle to a bicycle to a racing bike. All are cycles but the quality of distinction is obvious.

As with the three previous Realms, this one can appear at the time to be as far as one can go in subtlety of experience. The solidity of the old world-view gets shaken up again through such an experience. There is nowhere to hang one's hat. This Realm lacks formation of mind and perception. There is a silence in this Realm, free from thoughts, emotions and the upsurge of religious, and psychological experiences. They cannot enter or get close to this

Realm. The palpable silence of it renders irrelevant all direct experiences. Heart, mind and consciousness fade away.

Letting go of the previous Realms makes available the Realm of Neither Perception nor Non-perception. It is inappropriate to say in this Realm that there is still a knowing. It is equally inappropriate to speak of this state in unconscious terms.

We need not preoccupy ourselves with gaining such experiences. They may arise spontaneously. But generally we need guidance from those who have experienced and understood the Four Absorptions and Four Formless Realms. Even if we don't touch upon these Realms, we can still experience much insight, self-understanding and receptivity along the way.

The shift that neither confirms nor denies perception also correspondingly neither confirms nor denies what we perceive. It is hardly surprising that some teachers give the experience an ultimate status. It is not unusual in contemplative traditions that we set great store on this Realm. It reveals a different dimension of things altogether. Remembering the sublime nature of the Realm of Neither Perception nor Non-perception, the subsequent re-entry into the field of perceptions seems a step backwards. The substantial view of perception decreases in this Fourth Formless Realm. Right understanding acknowledges the way differences in perception change our whole view of the world.

Absorptions and the Realms will leave a bitter taste later if the self, the *I*, clings to any of them. It is a blessing to make contact with these Realms, to partake of utterly fresh and mystical experiences. They are not dreamed up, not a product of fantasy or thought. There is no doubt of their validity. We appreciate the way our life becomes enriched through contact with the Absorptions and the Formless Realms. But they are impermanent experiences.

There is something that matters more than the Absorptions and the Realms. That is liberation. The Four Absorptions and the Four Formless Realms indicate the depths of calmness, clarity and shifts in perception. The dedicated meditator, devoted to exploring an awakened life, may touch upon any of these levels. There are many teachers who believe that any one of these eight depths reveals an experience of the ultimate truth. They then train their students in the methods and techniques to acquire such experiences.

Other teachers point to the limitations of the Four Absorptions and the Four Formless Realms. Instead, they elevate the cessation of mind and body as the penultimate state, or talk of another experience as the transcendent one. They refer to this as Nirvana, or the final liberation. When a student has had such an experience and mastered it, the teacher often invites the student to become a teacher. This happened to the Buddha. He declined to teach the Formless Realms as the consummation of the Path. The same invitation has been extended to other experienced yogis, Eastern and Western, before and since. Loyal to their teachers, some students then point the way to Absorptions, formlessness or cessation as the confirmation of liberation.

What is true wisdom? What is Nirvana? It is not the quality of experience that matters but the insight and understanding. Authentic insight reveals an unshakeable freedom. We also realise the emptiness of problematic existence. An enlightened life cannot be lost. Despite its immense value, the experience of the Realm of Neither Perception nor Non-perception fades.

FOUR NOBLE ONES

This unwoven realm, not far, not near,
Nor in between; not above, not below;
Not revealed, not hidden;
Not solid, not insubstantial;
Not words, not silence,
Before which this ego collapses.

Introduction

The Four Noble Ones represent the consummation of the teachings. All the teachings and practices point to enlightenment. It is this enlightenment that reveals a Noble One. The major fruit of the Dharma comes through the realisation of liberation, that ends suffering, confusion and disatisfaction.

The Four Noble Ones are:

1. Stream-enterer.

2. Once-returner.

3. Non-returner.

4. *Arahant.*

Nobility emerges out of realisation, not from birth, marriage or titles. The Noble Ones all share something in common – they are grounded in the Dharma of the Unshakeable. They know profound friendship towards all forms of life. They have ceased to live in the duality of hungering for victory over defeat, success over failure. They do not cling to yesterday, today or tomorrow. They know a freedom that is indestructible.

Noble Ones do not rely upon a saviour, a sacred book or a transcendent God for their illumination. They do not grasp on to the view that such nobility arises solely through association with a teacher, personal effort or meditation.

Noble Ones remain reluctant to make claims about their realisations. For the *I* to make such claims can put into question liberation and its natural connection with the vast web of life. Life does not belong to self, to *I* and *my*. It belongs to the nature of things. Knowing this brings joy. The Noble Ones know a profound sense of fulfilment through life's journey.

We recognise Noble Ones through their way of being in the world and their steadfastness in times of trouble. There may be still some signs or outbursts of selfishness, negativity and fear for the Stream-enterer and to a much lesser extent for the Once-returner. The Non-returner knows the conceited *I* and restlessness, and gets attached to formless experiences. But Noble Ones have lost any appetite to feed unwholesome patterns. The *Arahant* remains unfettered to anything anywhere.

The *personality* of a Noble One varies. The personality of one may appear strict. Another may appear as the embodiment of kindness and humility. Another may have a sharpened mind that cuts through superficiality. They regard opinions about personality as empty.

Noble Ones know they have no life of their own. The notion of *having* a mind and body seems superficial in the extreme. Noble Ones pay respect to life while remaining free from giving value to selfishness.

Stream-enterer

The Dharma offers a practical and direct approach to a fully enlightened life; it is a resource pointing directly to the full and unexcelled enlightenment of a human being. The Dharma is not something to cling to.

Stream-enterers are enlightened since they know authentic liberation, but they still have work to do on themselves. Their realisations and way of living make them Noble Ones. There is a *knowing* for Stream-enterers of this immeasurable and indestructible freedom in daily life. Unwelcome and unwanted states of mind may arise and may well need clear attention, but these mind-states have no power to eradicate the discovery of freedom. The sun shines whether clouds drift across the sun or not. Stream-enterers know the sweetness of living with the truth of things, the emptiness of the ego and the joy of freedom. Some will speak the language of finding God. Their sustained practices destine them for complete enlightenment, free from any remaining fetters or obstructions. Stream-entry indicates the first major turning point towards a fully enlightened life.

There are practical signs of such realisation. The knowing of liberation does not exist in a vacuum. This means that any inner change that takes place remains relatively steady. It is not easily overcome by the changing circumstances of day-to-day life. The signs are:

1. *There is commitment to ethical principles; there is no wish to harm or exploit.* The quality and level of awareness regarding this are deeply significant. The nature of dependent-arising circumstances is understood and the gap of *us* and *them* has dissolved dramatically. In a very real way, one often perceives others as oneself. This view affects one's heart, mind and activities – true morality belongs to realisation. There is an effortless acknowledgement and appreciation of the Five Precepts: they are not commandments nor pressures to define oneself in a particular way. The Stream-enterer understands the interconnectedness of things.

2. *There is no doubt.* Conflict and uncertainty no longer torture the mind. In sudden transformation, one may wonder what happened, what that was all about. The Stream-enterer may not be able to put such realisations into language or description. Thoughts may arise about the significance of the change or one may have some doubts about its long-term impact, but here there is freedom from doubt about freedom itself. One has tasted pure, fresh water. There is no doubt about it.

3. *There is the end of clinging, attachment, and identification with rites and rituals.* It is not unusual for teachings and practices to deteriorate into clinging to religious observances. Ceremonies, rituals, methods and techniques become a substitute for opening the heart, depths of *samadhi* and insight into liberation. We begin to imagine that our particular methodology guarantees the highest wisdom.

The method and techniques then matter more than the liberation from clinging to such forms. There are countless numbers of sincere people who become stuck with their particular form. They cannot see through it. The problem is over for the Stream-enterer.

4. *There is no more clinging to personality belief.* It is easy to become obsessed with our personality, our self. Our personality becomes an area of major attention. There is the desire to impress and please. We think that our personality is something that has an inherent existence to it. Through preoccupation with it we become narcissistic. Self-infatuated, we only want to talk about ourselves. Everyone and everything else becomes secondary. Seeing through this, the Stream-enterer does not give great significance to personality. One has seen much more deeply than that. Others may speak of our personality in various ways. They will isolate different aspects of the mind and make that a description of who we are, but in clarity and realisation there comes natural happiness and contentment. One is no longer thinking in terms of *me and my personality* and all the ego that involves.

5. *There is no falling into hell.* Hell is an acutely painful state of mind. There are far too many people living a tortured inner life. There is much despair, depression and evidence of abnormal psychology. It becomes hell when a person no longer has the inner resources to resolve a situation. Falling into the pits of unhappiness is hell. The Stream-enterer cannot fall into such a hell. There is a sufficient degree of inner well-being to stop that from ever happening. Clarity and freedom become one's refuge. Consciousness is steadfast and supported with wisdom, and this brings confidence and understanding, diminishing the chance for any descent into hell.

6. *The Stream-enterer can still experience unresolved issues.* There is no hiding behind roles or acting through large layers of ego. Faults and failings do not remain hidden. The question often arises, 'How then can I know a liberated person? How do I know that there are such people on this earth?' It is easy to draw conclusions, favourable and unfavourable, about the realisations and attainments of certain people. Sometimes we measure people by the amount of good they do, their warmth and kindness or their clarity of mind. We cannot draw quick conclusions.

We must have a long-term association with somebody we

regard as liberated. It is folly to ignore their wisdom. We may become impressed with a guru or charismatic figure, and with very little contact build up a picture of this person. Time and close contact will tell whether he or she lives a noble life or not.

How does that person deal with a difficult situation or respond to a crisis? How do they deal with personal health or life-and-death issues? Stream-enterers know the sweetness of the non-duality of life and death, presence and absence, coming and going. Stream-entry reveals the knowing of inner freedom and any patterns and inner conditions to work on. Awareness reveals this without producing a conflict. The mind is truly vast, deep and immeasurable. The waves belong to the ocean. The Stream-enterer knows what is what. It is this clarity and its practice that brings complete fulfilment in the journey to Arahantship.

Once-returner

We recognise the value of making outer changes in our life. We rarely give the same consideration to the significance of genuine and profound inner change.

The essential concern of the Noble Ones involves transformation, and understanding the ultimate and relative truth of things. The ultimate truth stands steady, is unborn, unmade, unconditioned, uncreated and undying. It is available here and now, difficult to realise and obvious to the wise. Significant inner change makes available realisation of the ultimate truth that sets us free. Authentic inner change means the fading of the ego. The degree to which the ego dissolves is the degree to which the joy of emancipation reveals itself.

The Stream-enterer knows freedom as an authentic statement of fulfilment. There is a dramatic reduction in the grip of problematic existence upon consciousness. There is knowing of the Immeasurable. But there is still some residue of greed, anger and self-deception. The Once-returner has reduced this residue significantly compared to the Stream-enterer.

Some will imagine that the major change occurs in realisation of Stream-entry. They believe that once realisation has occurred, the rest is effortless change until the ego is totally exhausted. For the Noble Ones, the shifts from Stream-enterer to Once-returner and from Once-returner to Non-returner, and from Non-returner to *Arahant* are equally important. There is no sense of complacency. Just as a log flows downriver to the sea, if it does not get washed up on the bank, so the Stream-enterer flows to final freedom, but it still requires vigilance not to get caught on the bank of extremism. Stream-enterers retain a keen sense of liberating wisdom and insights. There is a passion and love of discovery, and of not returning to the forces of wanting and denying. The Once-returner has almost exhausted greed, anger and self-deception.

The Once-returner continues his or her dedication to the dissolution of all that is unsatisfactory within. The potency of each of the Five Hindrances gets challenged when any one of them, or combination of them, arises. This is not an obsessive attempt to make oneself perfect. It is a wise outlook. There is an understanding that these Hindrances influence the inner life and have an impact upon the world.

The work to dissolve them provides real support for others as much as ourselves. It is hardly surprising that one of the outstanding features of Noble Ones is their unfailing compassion, know as the *bodhisattva* mind. Such a mind shows itself in the solitary forest-dweller who takes care of every creature or plant. It also shows in the Noble Ones' dedication to lifelong service to others.

The Once-returner has no interest in blindly accepting the corrupting influence of unpleasant mind-states. Having known and tasted the sweetness of great liberation, there is no enthusiasm to fall back into the grip of unwelcome states of mind. The Noble Ones develop and explore the wide range of resources available for complete emancipation. There is use of meditation, reflection, practices and teachings for the resolution of all that may arise. The fading of anger and negativity does not take away constructive criticism. There is the freedom to express concerns clearly and directly. Others may misunderstand. They may think that criticism is negativity, moral concerns are self-righteousness and accountability means revenge, but these confusions do not apply to the perceptions of the Once-returner.

There is nothing passive about the Noble Ones' relationship to life. The dissolution of selfishness enhances the natural enjoyment of seeing, hearing, smelling, tasting, touching and what arises in consciousness. There is a depth of receptivity to joy rather than pursuit of personal pleasure. The heart and mind of the Once-returner stand steady like the truth itself. Such a person expresses immeasurable wisdom.

It is a delight to be in association with the Noble Ones. They know the finite appearance of this world. They feel no need to hold on to life because they can see through it. They embrace the totality of this diverse field of existence.

Non-returner

The Non-returner never returns to greed and anger. There is no more living with such expressions of self-deception. This brings a clear release from such matters, leaving only traces of ignorance, conceit, subtle clinging and restlessness for the Non-returner to dissolve to reach utter fulfilment of the teachings and practices.

By the time one reaches this stage, unwelcome states of mind have diminished considerably. These useless forces spring from the blindness of expectations and the excess of demands that we put upon ourselves and others. The Non-returner has negated such an unsatisfactory flow of conditioning. Even the ability to be in the subtle grip of a tendency is virtually exhausted for the Non-returner. There is very little left in the way of unsatisfactory conditioning of *I* and *my*. Wisdom prevents expectations leading to disappointment.

The concepts *Stream-enterer, Once-returner, Non-returner* and *Arahant* will appear awkward to those unfamiliar with them. They serve as definitions of states of realisation. They enable us to break away from the major problem associated with spiritual practices – the idea that one must become perfect. The Noble Ones live an enlightened life. They cling neither to notions of imperfection nor to perfection. They have abandoned these viewpoints. The Non-returner works with the ignorance and conceit involved in any views. His or her primary interest is full realisation, free from such unsatisfactory influences.

For example, there is the religious view that one can be saved. 'God has saved me' easily expresses a conceit of the self. For the realised ones, there is nothing to be saved or lost. The self experiences the pointlessness of building itself up on such stand-points or reacting against them. There is nothing to pursue or hold on to. Liberation is here and now. Grace is not an occasional hand-out from a selective transpersonal force. The Non-returner is one step away from complete, unexcelled liberation.

The Noble Ones know who they are. They may or may not place themselves into one of these four categories. Labels are not important to them. What is important is the wisdom of knowing the truth of things. Non-returners bring the light of awareness and insight to the last traces of the ego. Their compassion is all-embracing because they understand how states of mind bewitch people.

The Noble Ones barely concern themselves with personal desires. There is only a little significance in *I* for the the Non-returner. The Non-returner's ignorance manifests as blind spots in understanding. He or she can cling to the identity of being a Noble One. This shows conceit.

Non-returners regard experiences of ignorance and conceit as clouds obscuring bright sunlight shining through to the earth. Through insight, there is less momentum for the ego to rise again. It is this expansive and steady sense of great liberation that makes all the ardour of the teachings, disciplines and practices worth-while.

The Buddha teaches seven factors for enlightenment – aware-ness, Dharma inquiry, vitality, happiness, tranquillity, *samadhi* and equanimity. The Noble Ones know the liberating fruits of the Dharma life. The Non-returner has one stage left before ara-hantship and the complete fulfilment of the teachings.

The Noble Ones reveal the full potential of human existence. We should never underestimate the extraordinary significance of the Noble Ones in this world.

Arahant

To fulfil our capacity to see into life sets us free. Utterly free. Once and for all. Then there is an enlightened wisdom and joy about the whole process of life. There is no more grief and anguish, no more fear and indifference, no more confusion about the way things are.

We have seen through the world of birth, change, and death. Our mind is not a problem to us. We know that *I am* is a conceit. Such a one is an *Arahant*, who is fully liberated.

Yet our mind finds itself trapped in greed, negativity, fear and confusion. These psychological patterns distort our lives, actively preventing us from seeing clearly. What we have contact with are unsatisfactory states of mind. Wisdom only becomes available as we free the mind from such influential inner forces. The *Arahant* has ceased projecting all sorts of qualities and attributes on to objects and stands free from the conceit of a substantial self. The world of ego and all of its investments and compounded ideas have lost any significance. Unlike his noble predecessors, Stream-enterer, Once-returner and Non-returner, the *Arahant* has nothing more left to work on. He or she is free from living in a state of mental agitation, including longing for subtle experiences at any depth or realm.

The *Arahant* knows a freedom that goes beyond any kind of measurement. Nothing whatsoever can take this sublime liberation away. The comprehensive nature of such understanding shows itself in timeless understanding, natural joy and love. To see and know things as they truly are is to know liberation. To know liberation is to see and know things as they are. The so-called problems of life have gone for good.

The old Thai monk was dying. There was a quiet acknowledgement amongst some of those around him that he was an *Arahant*. He led a selfless existence in our monastery. When he spoke other monks listened with rapt attention. A few weeks before he died, I said to him, 'It won't be long before King Yama [the Lord of Death] comes looking for you. How do you feel about that?'

The old monk turned to me with a smile and said, 'King Yama has searched all over this earth looking for me. But he cannot find me anywhere. This monk is not to be found here nor there nor in-between.' On the morning he died I was on the alms round in the nearby village. He sent a monk to fetch me. I lay beside him on the mat on the floor in his hut while he died. At the end, he said: 'Seeing gone. Listening gone. All complete.' Then consciousness dissolved.

Being enlightened, the *Arahant* has broken through the world

216

of life and death. This awakening triggers extraordinary realisations and a generosity of spirit that remains undiminished. Death
loses its sting. The notion of becoming, and fear of the end of it,
gets swept away in these realisations. The *I* has as much significance as a line drawn on water.

There is the ordinary view and the trans-ordinary view. The
ordinary view says that we never stop evolving. There are some
who will proclaim that there is no end, that we are always changing
and evolving as a human being. What is important here is understanding the difference between the need to grow and develop and
knowing the end of the Dharma journey.

There is always much to learn. We believe we ought to cultivate
and sustain this attitude right until the last breath of our life. It
would seem conceited to claim that one has come to the end of the
evolutionary process, reached the completion of all becoming.
Others may say of the *Arahant*, 'Oh, he [or she] is growing. He has
changed over the years. He has greater insights/is a more loving
person/has a strengthening presence.' But this is the perception of
others. It has little or no meaning for the liberated one.

Any apparent developments of heart and mind occur through
the impulses of life rather than through having to make an effort to
be a better person. From a conventional perspective, an *Arahant*
also grows, changes his or her mind and becomes receptive to new
areas of life. Apparent modifications of the inner life are of little
importance to the *Arahant*.

Liberation ends becoming, ends clinging to views, ends comparing past to present, ends notions of personal survival or otherwise after death. Issues of self lose all their meaning. The picture
we carry of the self in the world does not belong to reality but to the
determinations of the mind. The picture we carry of the world does
not belong to the world.

The *Arahant* sees through the debate of one life or many lives
since he or she is free from location in or outside any of the Five
Aggregates. In this there is no location anywhere for *I and my life*
or *I and my death*. The *Arahant* is untraceable here and now and he
or she knows it. The problem of existence and non-existence, life
and death, has dissolved. The *Arahant* knows intimately a trans-
ordinary understanding.

The *Arahant* has done what has to be done, laid down the dif-

217

ficulties and burdens. There is an indestructible freedom. The *Arahant* has exhausted all karma, the unsatisfactory influences from the past. Victory and defeat, success and failure have no inherent significance. The truth, namely that which sets us free, neither expands, nor contracts, stands still, nor moves. It remains unaffected by the fluctuating circumstances of events between birth and death, including them both. The *Arahant* knows this. *Arahants* rest in the timeless Dharma of all things.

It doesn't matter whether one believes complete liberation is possible or not. It is not a subject for dogma or speculation. It is a matter of realisation. The end of suffering reveals the end of all clinging. Liberation is incomparable.

May all beings live in peace.
May all beings be liberated.
May all beings realise a fully enlightened life.

For further information about retreats offering Dharma teachings and Insight Meditation please write to:

Insight Meditation Society
1230 Pleasant Street
Barre, MA 01005
(978) 355-4378

Spirit Rock Meditation Center
P.O. Box 909
5000 Sir Francis Drake Blvd.
Woodacre, CA 94973
(415) 488-0164

Gaia House Trust
West Ogwell
near Newton Abbot
Devon TQ9 6EN
England
tel: 44 (0) 1626 333613
fax: 44 (0) 1626 352650
e-mail: gaiahouse@gn.apc.org
World Wide Web Pages:
http://www.gn.apc.org/gaiahouse
http//www.insightmeditation.org

ABOUT THE AUTHOR

Christopher Titmuss is the co-founder of one of the largest and most respected retreat centres in the UK, from where he travels all over the world to teach Awakening and Insight Meditation retreats. From 1962 to 1967 he worked as a reporter and photojournalist in London, Turkey, Thailand, Laos and Australia – and then spent six years as a Buddhist monk in Thailand and India. For the last twenty years he has been teaching the Dharma. He is an active supporter of global responsibility and is a founder member of the twelve-strong international board of the Buddhist Peace Fellowship. In 1986 and 1992 he stood for Parliament for the Green Party.